Includes
ICD-9-CM
Codes
Effective
1-Oct-96

DIAGNOSTIC
CRITERIA
FROM
DSM-IV™

Includes
ICD-9-CM
Codes
Effective
1-Oct-96

Diagnostic

Criteria

From

DSM-IV™

Published by the
American Psychiatric Association
Washington, DC

Manufactured in the United States of America on acid-free paper

American Psychiatric Association
1400 K Street, N.W., Washington, DC 20005

DSM and DSM-IV are trademarks of the American Psychiatric Association. Use of these terms is prohibited without permission of the American Psychiatric Association.

Correspondence regarding copyright permissions should be directed to the Division of Publications and Marketing, American Psychiatric Association, 1400 K Street, N.W., Washington, DC 20005.

Citations of diagnostic criteria and other text should be made by referring to the main edition of this work. The correct citation is American Psychiatric Association: *Diagnostic and Statistical Manual of Mental Disorders,* Fourth Edition. Washington, DC, American Psychiatric Association, 1994.

ISBN 0-89042-063-7—Quick Reference
ISBN 0-89042-064-5—Desk Reference

First printing, May 1994
Second printing, July 1994
Third printing, January 1995
Fourth printing, December 1996—includes ICD-9-CM codes
   effective October 1, 1996
Fifth printing, July 1998
Sixth printing, April 1999

To Melvin Sabshin,
a man for all seasons

Contents

Introduction

One of the most important features of DSM-IV is its provision of diagnostic criteria to improve the reliability of diagnostic judgments. For quick reference, the clinician may wish to have available a small and convenient manual that contains only the DSM-IV Classification and diagnostic criteria sets. This "Mini-D" is meant to be used in conjunction with DSM-IV. Its proper use requires familiarity with the text descriptions for each disorder that accompany the criteria sets in DSM-IV.

Allen Frances, M.D.
Chair,
Task Force on DSM-IV

Harold Alan Pincus, M.D.
Vice-Chair,
Task Force on DSM-IV

Michael B. First, M.D.
Editor,
DSM-IV Text and Criteria

Thomas A. Widiger, Ph.D.
Research Coordinator

Cautionary Statement

The specified diagnostic criteria for each mental disorder are offered as guidelines for making diagnoses, because it has been demonstrated that the use of such criteria enhances agreement among clinicians and investigators. The proper use of these criteria requires specialized clinical training that provides both a body of knowledge and clinical skills.

These diagnostic criteria and the DSM-IV Classification of mental disorders reflect a consensus of current formulations of evolving knowledge in our field. They do not encompass, however, all the conditions for which people may be treated or that may be appropriate topics for research efforts.

The purpose of DSM-IV is to provide clear descriptions of diagnostic categories in order to enable clinicians and investigators to diagnose, communicate about, study, and treat people with various mental disorders. It is to be understood that inclusion here, for clinical and research purposes, of a diagnostic category such as Pathological Gambling or Pedophilia does not imply that the condition meets legal or other nonmedical criteria for what constitutes mental disease, mental disorder, or mental disability. The clinical and scientific considerations involved in categorization of these conditions as mental disorders may not be wholly relevant to legal judgments, for example, that take into account such issues as individual responsibility, disability determination, and competency.

Use of the Manual

Note: The reader should refer to the "Use of the Manual" section in DSM-IV (p. 1) for a more complete discussion.

Diagnostic Codes

The official coding system in use in the United States as of publication of this manual is the *International Classification of Diseases,* Ninth Revision, Clinical Modification (ICD-9-CM). Most DSM-IV disorders have a numerical ICD-9-CM code that precedes the name of the disorder in the Classification and accompanies the criteria set for each disorder. For some diagnoses (e.g., Mental Retardation, Substance-Induced Mood Disorder), the appropriate code depends on further specification and is listed after the criteria set for the disorder. The names of some disorders are followed by alternative terms enclosed in parentheses, which, in most cases, were the DSM-III-R names for the disorders.

Subtypes (some of which are coded in the fifth digit) and specifiers are provided for increased specificity. *Subtypes* define mutually exclusive and jointly exhaustive phenomenological subgroupings within a diagnosis and are indicated by the instruction "specify type" in the criteria set. For example, Delusional Disorder is subtyped based on the content of the delusions, with seven subtypes provided: Erotomanic Type, Grandiose Type, Jealous Type, Persecutory Type, Somatic Type, Mixed Type, and Unspecified Type. In contrast, *specifiers* are not intended to be mutually exclusive or jointly exhaustive and are indicated by the instruction "specify" or "specify if" in the criteria set (e.g., for Social Phobia, the instruction notes "Specify if: Generalized"). Specifiers provide an opportunity to define a more homogeneous subgrouping of individuals with the disorder who share certain features (e.g., Major Depressive Disorder, With Melancholic Features). Although a fifth digit is sometimes assigned to code a subtype or specifier (e.g., 290.12 Dementia of the Alzheimer's Type, With Early Onset, With Delusions) or severity (296.21 Major Depressive Disorder, Single Episode, Mild), the majority of subtypes and specifiers included in DSM-IV cannot be coded within the ICD-9-CM system and are indicated only by including the subtype or specifier after the name of the disorder (e.g., Social Phobia, Generalized).

Severity and Course Specifiers

A DSM-IV diagnosis is usually applied to the individual's current presentation and is not typically used to denote previous diagnoses from which the individual has recovered. The following specifiers indicating severity and course may be listed after the diagnosis: Mild, Moderate, Severe, In Partial Remission, In Full Remission, and Prior History.

The specifiers Mild, Moderate, and Severe should be used only when the full criteria for the disorder are currently met. In deciding whether the presentation should be described as mild, moderate, or severe, the clinician should take into account the number and intensity of the signs and symptoms of the disorder and any resulting impairment in occupational or social functioning. For the majority of disorders, the following guidelines may be used:

Mild.   Few, if any, symptoms in excess of those required to make the diagnosis are present, and symptoms result in no more than minor impairment in social or occupational functioning.

Moderate. Symptoms or functional impairment between "mild" and "severe" are present.

Severe. Many symptoms in excess of those required to make the diagnosis, or several symptoms that are particularly severe, are present, or the symptoms result in marked impairment in social or occupational functioning.

In Partial Remission. The full criteria for the disorder were previously met, but currently only some of the symptoms or signs of the disorder remain.

In Full Remission. There are no longer any symptoms or signs of the disorder, but it is still clinically relevant to note the disorder—for example, in an individual with previous episodes of Bipolar Disorder who has been symptom free on lithium for the past 3 years. After a period of time in full remission, the clinician may judge the individual to be recovered and, therefore, would no longer code the disorder as a current diagnosis. The differentiation of In Full Remission from recovered requires consideration of many factors, including the characteristic course of the disorder, the length of time since the last period of disturbance, the total duration of the disturbance, and the need for continued evaluation or prophylactic treatment.

Prior History. For some purposes, it may be useful to note a history of the criteria having been met for a disorder even when the individual is considered to be recovered from it. Such past diagnoses of mental disorder would be indicated by using the specifier Prior History (e.g., Separation Anxiety Disorder, Prior History, for an individual with a history of Separation Anxiety Disorder who has no current disorder or who currently meets criteria for Panic Disorder).

Specific criteria for defining Mild, Moderate, and Severe have been provided for the following: Mental Retardation, Conduct Disorder, Manic Episode, and Major Depressive Episode. Specific criteria for defining In Partial Remission and In Full Remission have been provided for the following: Manic Episode, Major Depressive Episode, and Substance Dependence.

Recurrence

Not infrequently in clinical practice, individuals after a period of time in which the full criteria for the disorder are no longer met (i.e., in partial or full remission or recovery) may develop symptoms that suggest a recurrence of their original disorder but that do not yet meet the full threshold for that disorder as specified in the criteria set. It is a matter of clinical judgment as to how best to indicate the presence of these symptoms. The following options are available:

- If the symptoms are judged to be a new episode of a recurrent condition, the disorder may be diagnosed as current (or provisional) even before the full criteria have been met (e.g., after meeting criteria for a Major Depressive Episode for only 10 days instead of the 14 days usually required).
- If the symptoms are judged to be clinically significant but it is not clear whether they constitute a recurrence of the original disorder, the appropriate Not Otherwise Specified category may be given.
- If it is judged that the symptoms are not clinically significant, no additional current or provisional diag-

nosis is given, but "Prior History" may be noted (see p. 3).

Principal Diagnosis/Reason for Visit

When more than one diagnosis for an individual is given in an inpatient setting, the *principal diagnosis* is the condition established after study to be chiefly responsible for occasioning the admission of the individual. When more than one diagnosis is given for an individual in an outpatient setting, the *reason for visit* is the condition that is chiefly responsible for the ambulatory care medical services received during the visit. In most cases, the principal diagnosis or the reason for visit is also the main focus of attention or treatment. It is often difficult (and somewhat arbitrary) to determine which diagnosis is the principal diagnosis or the reason for visit, especially in situations of "dual diagnosis" (a substance-related diagnosis like Amphetamine Dependence accompanied by a non-substance-related diagnosis like Schizophrenia). For example, it may be unclear which diagnosis should be considered "principal" for an individual hospitalized with both Schizophrenia and Amphetamine Intoxication, because each condition may have contributed equally to the need for admission and treatment.

Multiple diagnoses can be reported in a multiaxial fashion or in a nonaxial fashion. When the principal diagnosis is an Axis I disorder, this is indicated by listing it first. The remaining disorders are listed in order of focus of attention and treatment. When a person has both an Axis I and an Axis II diagnosis, the principal diagnosis or the reason for visit will be assumed to be on Axis I unless the Axis II diagnosis is followed by the qualifying phrase "(Principal Diagnosis)" or "(Reason for Visit)."

Provisional Diagnosis

The specifier *provisional* can be used when there is a strong presumption that the full criteria will ultimately be met for a disorder, but not enough information is available to make a firm diagnosis. The clinician can indicate the diagnostic uncertainty by recording "(Provisional)" following the diagnosis. For example, the individual appears to have a Major Depressive Disorder, but is unable to give an adequate history to establish that the full criteria are met. Another use of the term *provisional* is for those situations in which differential diagnosis depends exclusively on the duration of illness. For example, a diagnosis of Schizophreniform Disorder requires a duration of less than 6 months and can only be given provisionally if assigned before remission has occurred.

Use of Not Otherwise Specified Categories

Because of the diversity of clinical presentations, it is impossible for the diagnostic nomenclature to cover every possible situation. For this reason, each diagnostic class has at least one Not Otherwise Specified (NOS) category and some classes have several NOS categories. There are four situations in which an NOS diagnosis may be appropriate:

- The presentation conforms to the general guidelines for a mental disorder in the diagnostic class, but the symptomatic picture does not meet the criteria for any of the specific disorders. This would occur either when the symptoms are below the diagnostic threshold for one of the specific disorders or when there is an atypical or mixed presentation.

- The presentation conforms to a symptom pattern that has not been included in the DSM-IV Classification but that causes clinically significant distress or impairment. Research criteria for some of these symptom patterns have been included in Appendix B ("Criteria Sets and Axes Provided for Further Study") in DSM-IV.

- There is uncertainty about etiology (i.e., whether the disorder is due to a general medical condition, is substance induced, or is primary).

- There is insufficient opportunity for complete data collection (e.g., in emergency situations) or inconsistent or contradictory information, but there is enough information to place it within a particular diagnostic class (e.g., the clinician determines that the individual has psychotic symptoms but does not have enough information to diagnose a specific Psychotic Disorder).

DSM-IV Classification

NOS = Not Otherwise Specified.

An *x* appearing in a diagnostic code indicates that a specific code number is required.

An ellipsis (. . .) is used in the names of certain disorders to indicate that the name of a specific mental disorder or general medical condition should be inserted when recording the name (e.g., 293.0 Delirium Due to Hypothyroidism).

Numbers in parentheses are page numbers.

If criteria are currently met, one of the following severity specifiers may be noted after the diagnosis:

    Mild
    Moderate
    Severe

If criteria are no longer met, one of the following specifiers may be noted:

    In Partial Remission
    In Full Remission
    Prior History

Disorders Usually First Diagnosed in Infancy, Childhood, or Adolescence (49)

MENTAL RETARDATION (50)

Note: *These are coded on Axis II.*

317	Mild Mental Retardation (50)
318.0	Moderate Mental Retardation (50)
318.1	Severe Mental Retardation (50)
318.2	Profound Mental Retardation (50)
319	Mental Retardation, Severity Unspecified (51)

LEARNING DISORDERS (51)

315.00	Reading Disorder (51)
315.1	Mathematics Disorder (51)
315.2	Disorder of Written Expression (52)
315.9	Learning Disorder NOS (52)

MOTOR SKILLS DISORDER (53)

315.4	Developmental Coordination Disorder (53)

COMMUNICATION DISORDERS (54)

315.31	Expressive Language Disorder (54)
315.32	Mixed Receptive-Expressive Language Disorder (55)
315.39	Phonological Disorder (55)
307.0	Stuttering (56)
307.9	Communication Disorder NOS (57)

PERVASIVE DEVELOPMENTAL DISORDERS (57)

299.00	Autistic Disorder (57)
299.80	Rett's Disorder (59)
299.10	Childhood Disintegrative Disorder (60)
299.80	Asperger's Disorder (61)
299.80	Pervasive Developmental Disorder NOS (62)

307.6   Enuresis (Not Due to a General Medical
         Condition) (74)
         Specify type: Nocturnal Only/Diurnal Only/Nocturnal and
         Diurnal

OTHER DISORDERS OF INFANCY, CHILDHOOD, OR ADOLESCENCE (75)

309.21   Separation Anxiety Disorder (75)
          Specify if: Early Onset
313.23   Selective Mutism (76)
313.89   Reactive Attachment Disorder of Infancy or Early
          Childhood (77)
          Specify type: Inhibited Type/Disinhibited Type
307.3   Stereotypic Movement Disorder (78)
          Specify if: With Self-Injurious Behavior

313.9   Disorder of Infancy, Childhood, or
          Adolescence NOS (79)

Delirium, Dementia, and Amnestic and Other Cognitive Disorders (81)

DELIRIUM (81)

293.0   Delirium Due to . . . *[Indicate the General Medical
          Condition]* (81)
——.–   Substance Intoxication Delirium *(refer to
          Substance-Related Disorders for substance-
          specific codes)* (82)
——.–   Substance Withdrawal Delirium *(refer to
          Substance-Related Disorders for substance-
          specific codes)* (83)
——.–   Delirium Due to Multiple Etiologies *(code each
          of the specific etiologies)* (84)
780.09   Delirium NOS (85)

DEMENTIA (85)

290.xx   Dementia of the Alzheimer's Type, With Early
             Onset *(also code 331.0 Alzheimer's disease on
             Axis III)* (85)

   .10   Uncomplicated
   .11   With Delirium
   .12   With Delusions
   .13   With Depressed Mood
             Specify if: With Behavioral Disturbance

290.xx   Dementia of the Alzheimer's Type, With Late
             Onset *(also code 331.0 Alzheimer's disease on
             Axis III)* (85)

   .0   Uncomplicated
   .3   With Delirium
   .20   With Delusions
   .21   With Depressed Mood
             Specify if: With Behavioral Disturbance

290.xx   Vascular Dementia (88)
   .40   Uncomplicated
   .41   With Delirium
   .42   With Delusions
   .43   With Depressed Mood
             Specify if: With Behavioral Disturbance

294.1   Dementia Due to HIV Disease *(also code 042
             HIV infection affecting central nervous system on
             Axis III)* (90)

294.1   Dementia Due to Head Trauma *(also code 854.00
             head injury on Axis III)* (90)

294.1   Dementia Due to Parkinson's Disease *(also code
             332.0 Parkinson's disease on Axis III)* (90)

294.1   Dementia Due to Huntington's Disease *(also code
             333.4 Huntington's disease on Axis III)* (90)

290.10   Dementia Due to Pick's Disease *(also code 331.1
             Pick's disease on Axis III)* (90)

Mental Disorders Due to a General Medical Condition Not Elsewhere Classified (97)

293.9   Mental Disorder NOS Due to . . . *[Indicate the General Medical Condition]* (100)

Substance-Related Disorders (103)

[a]*The following specifiers may be applied to Substance Dependence:*

With Physiological Dependence/Without Physiological Dependence

Early Full Remission/Early Partial Remission
Sustained Full Remission/Sustained Partial Remission
On Agonist Therapy/In a Controlled Environment

The following specifiers apply to Substance-Induced Disorders as noted:
[I]With Onset During Intoxication/[W]With Onset During Withdrawal

ALCOHOL-RELATED DISORDERS (116)
Alcohol Use Disorders (116)
303.90   Alcohol Dependence[a] (108)
305.00   Alcohol Abuse (112)

Alcohol-Induced Disorders (116)
303.00   Alcohol Intoxication (117)
291.81   Alcohol Withdrawal (118)
             Specify if: With Perceptual Disturbances
291.0   Alcohol Intoxication Delirium (82)
291.0   Alcohol Withdrawal Delirium (83)
291.2   Alcohol-Induced Persisting Dementia (91)
291.1   Alcohol-Induced Persisting Amnestic Disorder (94)
291.x   Alcohol-Induced Psychotic Disorder (157)
    .5   With Delusions[I,W]
    .3   With Hallucinations[I,W]
291.89   Alcohol-Induced Mood Disorder[I,W] (184)

291.89   Alcohol-Induced Anxiety Disorder[I,W] (215)
291.89   Alcohol-Induced Sexual Dysfunction[I] (240)
291.89   Alcohol-Induced Sleep Disorder[I,W] (266)

291.9   Alcohol-Related Disorder NOS (117)

AMPHETAMINE (OR AMPHETAMINE-LIKE)–RELATED DISORDERS (119)

Amphetamine Use Disorders (119)

304.40   Amphetamine Dependence[a] (108)
305.70   Amphetamine Abuse (112)

Amphetamine-Induced Disorders (119)

292.89   Amphetamine Intoxication (120)
          Specify if: With Perceptual Disturbances
292.0   Amphetamine Withdrawal (121)
292.81   Amphetamine Intoxication Delirium (82)
292.xx   Amphetamine-Induced Psychotic Disorder (157)
    .11   With Delusions[I]
    .12   With Hallucinations[I]
292.84   Amphetamine-Induced Mood Disorder[I,W] (184)
292.89   Amphetamine-Induced Anxiety Disorder[I] (215)
292.89   Amphetamine-Induced Sexual Dysfunction[I] (240)
292.89   Amphetamine-Induced Sleep Disorder[I,W] (266)

292.9   Amphetamine-Related Disorder NOS (120)

CAFFEINE-RELATED DISORDERS (122)

Caffeine-Induced Disorders (122)

305.90   Caffeine Intoxication (123)
292.89   Caffeine-Induced Anxiety Disorder[I] (215)
292.89   Caffeine-Induced Sleep Disorder[I] (266)

292.9   Caffeine-Related Disorder NOS (122)

CANNABIS-RELATED DISORDERS (123)

Cannabis Use Disorders (123)

304.30   Cannabis Dependence[a] (108)
305.20   Cannabis Abuse (112)

Cannabis-Induced Disorders (124)

292.89   Cannabis Intoxication (124)
          Specify if: With Perceptual Disturbances
292.81   Cannabis Intoxication Delirium (82)
292.xx   Cannabis-Induced Psychotic Disorder (157)
   .11   With Delusions[I]
   .12   With Hallucinations[I]
292.89   Cannabis-Induced Anxiety Disorder[I] (215)

292.9   Cannabis-Related Disorder NOS (124)

COCAINE-RELATED DISORDERS (125)

Cocaine Use Disorders (125)

304.20   Cocaine Dependence[a] (108)
305.60   Cocaine Abuse (112)

Cocaine-Induced Disorders (125)

292.89   Cocaine Intoxication (126)
          Specify if: With Perceptual Disturbances
292.0   Cocaine Withdrawal (128)
292.81   Cocaine Intoxication Delirium (82)
292.xx   Cocaine-Induced Psychotic Disorder (157)
   .11   With Delusions[I]
   .12   With Hallucinations[I]
292.84   Cocaine-Induced Mood Disorder[I,W] (184)
292.89   Cocaine-Induced Anxiety Disorder[I,W] (215)
292.89   Cocaine-Induced Sexual Dysfunction[I] (240)
292.89   Cocaine-Induced Sleep Disorder[I,W] (266)

292.9   Cocaine-Related Disorder NOS (126)

HALLUCINOGEN-RELATED DISORDERS (128)

Hallucinogen Use Disorders (128)

304.50   Hallucinogen Dependence[a] (108)
305.30   Hallucinogen Abuse (112)

Hallucinogen-Induced Disorders (128)

292.89   Hallucinogen Intoxication (129)
292.89   Hallucinogen Persisting Perception Disorder
               (Flashbacks) (130)
292.81   Hallucinogen Intoxication Delirium (82)
292.xx   Hallucinogen-Induced Psychotic Disorder (157)
     .11   With Delusions[I]
     .12   With Hallucinations[I]
292.84   Hallucinogen-Induced Mood Disorder[I] (184)
292.89   Hallucinogen-Induced Anxiety Disorder[I] (215)

292.9   Hallucinogen-Related Disorder NOS (129)

INHALANT-RELATED DISORDERS (131)

Inhalant Use Disorders (131)

304.60   Inhalant Dependence[a] (108)
305.90   Inhalant Abuse (112)

Inhalant-Induced Disorders (131)

292.89   Inhalant Intoxication (132)
292.81   Inhalant Intoxication Delirium (82)
292.82   Inhalant-Induced Persisting Dementia (91)
292.xx   Inhalant-Induced Psychotic Disorder (157)
     .11   With Delusions[I]
     .12   With Hallucinations[I]
292.84   Inhalant-Induced Mood Disorder[I] (184)
292.89   Inhalant-Induced Anxiety Disorder[I] (215)

292.9   Inhalant-Related Disorder NOS (132)

NICOTINE-RELATED DISORDERS (133)

Nicotine Use Disorder (133)
305.10   Nicotine Dependence[a] (108)

Nicotine-Induced Disorder (133)
292.0   Nicotine Withdrawal (133)

292.9   Nicotine-Related Disorder NOS (133)

OPIOID-RELATED DISORDERS (134)

Opioid Use Disorders (134)
304.00   Opioid Dependence[a] (108)
305.50   Opioid Abuse (112)

Opioid-Induced Disorders (134)
292.89   Opioid Intoxication (135)
          Specify if: With Perceptual Disturbances
292.0   Opioid Withdrawal (136)
292.81   Opioid Intoxication Delirium (82)
292.xx   Opioid-Induced Psychotic Disorder (157)
    .11   With Delusions[I]
    .12   With Hallucinations[I]
292.84   Opioid-Induced Mood Disorder[I] (184)
292.89   Opioid-Induced Sexual Dysfunction[I] (240)
292.89   Opioid-Induced Sleep Disorder[I,W] (266)

292.9   Opioid-Related Disorder NOS (135)

PHENCYCLIDINE (OR PHENCYCLIDINE-LIKE)– RELATED DISORDERS (137)

Phencyclidine Use Disorders (137)
304.60   Phencyclidine Dependence[a] (108)
305.90   Phencyclidine Abuse (112)

Phencyclidine-Induced Disorders (137)

292.89   Phencyclidine Intoxication (138)
          Specify if: With Perceptual Disturbances
292.81   Phencyclidine Intoxication Delirium (82)
292.xx   Phencyclidine-Induced Psychotic Disorder (157)
    .11   With Delusions[I]
    .12   With Hallucinations[I]
292.84   Phencyclidine-Induced Mood Disorder[I] (184)
292.89   Phencyclidine-Induced Anxiety Disorder[I] (215)

292.9   Phencyclidine-Related Disorder NOS (138)

SEDATIVE-, HYPNOTIC-, OR ANXIOLYTIC-RELATED DISORDERS (139)

Sedative, Hypnotic, or Anxiolytic Use Disorders (139)

304.10   Sedative, Hypnotic, or Anxiolytic
          Dependence[a] (108)
305.40   Sedative, Hypnotic, or Anxiolytic Abuse (112)

Sedative-, Hypnotic-, or Anxiolytic-Induced Disorders (139)

292.89   Sedative, Hypnotic, or Anxiolytic
          Intoxication (141)
292.0   Sedative, Hypnotic, or Anxiolytic
          Withdrawal (142)
          Specify if: With Perceptual Disturbances
292.81   Sedative, Hypnotic, or Anxiolytic Intoxication
          Delirium (82)
292.81   Sedative, Hypnotic, or Anxiolytic Withdrawal
          Delirium (83)
292.82   Sedative-, Hypnotic-, or Anxiolytic-Induced
          Persisting Dementia (91)
292.83   Sedative-, Hypnotic-, or Anxiolytic-Induced
          Persisting Amnestic Disorder (94)

POLYSUBSTANCE-RELATED DISORDER (143)

OTHER (OR UNKNOWN) SUBSTANCE–RELATED DISORDERS (143)

Other (or Unknown) Substance Use Disorders (144)

Other (or Unknown) Substance–Induced Disorders (144)

Schizophrenia and Other Psychotic Disorders (147)

The following Classification of Longitudinal Course applies to all subtypes of Schizophrenia:

Episodic With Interepisode Residual Symptoms (*specify if:* With
    Prominent Negative Symptoms)/Episodic With No Interepisode
    Residual Symptoms
Continuous (*specify if:* With Prominent Negative Symptoms)
Single Episode In Partial Remission (*specify if:* With Prominent
    Negative Symptoms)/Single Episode In Full Remission
Other or Unspecified Pattern

.20	Catatonic Type (149)
.90	Undifferentiated Type (150)
.60	Residual Type (150)

295.40 Schizophreniform Disorder (152)
Specify if: Without Good Prognostic Features/With Good Prognostic Features

295.70 Schizoaffective Disorder (152)
Specify type: Bipolar Type/Depressive Type

297.1 Delusional Disorder (153)
Specify type: Erotomanic Type/Grandiose Type/Jealous Type/Persecutory Type/Somatic Type/Mixed Type/Unspecified Type

298.8 Brief Psychotic Disorder (154)
Specify if: With Marked Stressor(s)/Without Marked Stressor(s)/With Postpartum Onset

297.3 Shared Psychotic Disorder (155)

293.xx Psychotic Disorder Due to . . . *[Indicate the General Medical Condition]* (156)

    .81 With Delusions

    .82 With Hallucinations

——.– Substance-Induced Psychotic Disorder *(refer to Substance-Related Disorders for substance-specific codes)* (157)
Specify if: With Onset During Intoxication/With Onset During Withdrawal

298.9 Psychotic Disorder NOS (159)

Mood Disorders (161)

Code current state of Major Depressive Disorder or Bipolar I Disorder in fifth digit:

1 = Mild
2 = Moderate
3 = Severe Without Psychotic Features

4 = Severe With Psychotic Features
        Specify: Mood-Congruent Psychotic
        Features/Mood-Incongruent Psychotic Features
5 = In Partial Remission
6 = In Full Remission
0 = Unspecified

The following specifiers apply (for current or most recent episode) to Mood Disorders as noted:

[a]Severity/Psychotic/Remission Specifiers/[b]Chronic/[c]With Catatonic Features/[d]With Melancholic Features/[e]With Atypical Features/[f]With Postpartum Onset

The following specifiers apply to Mood Disorders as noted:

[g]With or Without Full Interepisode Recovery/[h]With Seasonal Pattern/[i]With Rapid Cycling

DEPRESSIVE DISORDERS (167)

296.xx	Major Depressive Disorder,	
.2x	Single Episode[a,b,c,d,e,f] (167)	
.3x	Recurrent[a,b,c,d,e,f,g,h] (168)	
300.4	Dysthymic Disorder (169)	
	Specify if: Early Onset/Late Onset	
	Specify: With Atypical Features	
311	Depressive Disorder NOS (171)	

BIPOLAR DISORDERS (173)

296.xx	Bipolar I Disorder, (173)	
.0x	Single Manic Episode[a,c,f] (173)	
	Specify if: Mixed	
.40	Most Recent Episode Hypomanic[g,h,i] (174)	
.4x	Most Recent Episode Manic[a,c,f,g,h,i] (175)	
.6x	Most Recent Episode Mixed[a,c,f,g,h,i] (176)	
.5x	Most Recent Episode Depressed[a,b,c,d,e,f,g,h,i] (177)	
.7	Most Recent Episode Unspecified[g,h,i] (178)	

296.89   Bipolar II Disorder[a,b,c,d,e,f,g,h,i] (180)
           Specify (current or most recent episode):
           Hypomanic/Depressed
301.13   Cyclothymic Disorder (181)
296.80   Bipolar Disorder NOS (182)

293.83   Mood Disorder Due to . . . *[Indicate the General*
           Medical Condition] (183)
           Specify type: With Depressive Features/With Major
           Depressive–Like Episode/With Manic Features/With Mixed
           Features
——.—   Substance-Induced Mood Disorder *(refer to*
           Substance-Related Disorders for substance-
           specific codes) (184)
           Specify type: With Depressive Features/With Manic
           Features/With Mixed Features
           Specify if: With Onset During Intoxication/With Onset
           During Withdrawal

296.90   Mood Disorder NOS (186)

Anxiety Disorders (199)

300.01   Panic Disorder Without Agoraphobia (201)
300.21   Panic Disorder With Agoraphobia (202)
300.22   Agoraphobia Without History of Panic
           Disorder (203)
300.29   Specific Phobia (203)
           Specify type: Animal Type/Natural Environment Type/
           Blood-Injection-Injury Type/Situational Type/Other Type
300.23   Social Phobia (205)
           Specify if: Generalized
300.3   Obsessive-Compulsive Disorder (207)
           Specify if: With Poor Insight

Somatoform Disorders (219)

Factitious Disorders (227)

Dissociative Disorders (229)

Sexual and Gender Identity Disorders (233)

SEXUAL DYSFUNCTIONS (233)
The following specifiers apply to all primary Sexual Dysfunctions:

Lifelong Type/Acquired Type
Generalized Type/Situational Type
Due to Psychological Factors/Due to Combined Factors

Sexual Desire Disorders (233)

———.— Substance-Induced Sexual Dysfunction *(refer to Substance-Related Disorders for substance-specific codes)* (240)
Specify if: With Impaired Desire/With Impaired Arousal/With Impaired Orgasm/With Sexual Pain
Specify if: With Onset During Intoxication

302.70 Sexual Dysfunction NOS (242)

PARAPHILIAS (243)

302.4 Exhibitionism (243)
302.81 Fetishism (243)
302.89 Frotteurism (244)
302.2 Pedophilia (244)
Specify if: Sexually Attracted to Males/Sexually Attracted to Females/Sexually Attracted to Both
Specify if: Limited to Incest
Specify type: Exclusive Type/Nonexclusive Type
302.83 Sexual Masochism (245)
302.84 Sexual Sadism (245)
302.3 Transvestic Fetishism (245)
Specify if: With Gender Dysphoria
302.82 Voyeurism (246)
302.9 Paraphilia NOS (246)

GENDER IDENTITY DISORDERS (246)

302.xx Gender Identity Disorder (246)
  .6   in Children
  .85   in Adolescents or Adults
Specify if: Sexually Attracted to Males/Sexually Attracted to Females/Sexually Attracted to Both/Sexually Attracted to Neither
302.6 Gender Identity Disorder NOS (248)

302.9 Sexual Disorder NOS (249)

Eating Disorders (251)

307.1   Anorexia Nervosa (251)
          Specify type: Restricting Type; Binge-Eating/Purging Type
307.51   Bulimia Nervosa (252)
          Specify type: Purging Type/Nonpurging Type
307.50   Eating Disorder NOS (253)

Sleep Disorders (255)

PRIMARY SLEEP DISORDERS (255)

Dyssomnias (255)
307.42   Primary Insomnia (255)
307.44   Primary Hypersomnia (256)
          Specify if: Recurrent
347   Narcolepsy (257)
780.59   Breathing-Related Sleep Disorder (257)
307.45   Circadian Rhythm Sleep Disorder (258)
          Specify type: Delayed Sleep Phase Type/Jet Lag
          Type/Shift Work Type/Unspecified Type
307.47   Dyssomnia NOS (259)

Parasomnias (260)
307.47   Nightmare Disorder (260)
307.46   Sleep Terror Disorder (261)
307.46   Sleepwalking Disorder (261)
307.47   Parasomnia NOS (262)

SLEEP DISORDERS RELATED TO ANOTHER MENTAL DISORDER (263)
307.42   Insomnia Related to . . . *[Indicate the Axis I or
          Axis II Disorder]* (263)
307.44   Hypersomnia Related to . . . *[Indicate the Axis I or
          Axis II Disorder]* (264)

OTHER SLEEP DISORDERS (265)

780.xx	Sleep Disorder Due to . . . *[Indicate the General Medical Condition]* (265)
.52	Insomnia Type
.54	Hypersomnia Type
.59	Parasomnia Type
.59	Mixed Type
——.–	Substance-Induced Sleep Disorder *(refer to Substance-Related Disorders for substance-specific codes)* (266)

Specify type: Insomnia Type/Hypersomnia Type/ Parasomnia Type/Mixed Type
Specify if: With Onset During Intoxication/With Onset During Withdrawal

Impulse-Control Disorders Not Elsewhere Classified (269)

312.34	Intermittent Explosive Disorder (269)
312.32	Kleptomania (269)
312.33	Pyromania (270)
312.31	Pathological Gambling (271)
312.39	Trichotillomania (272)
312.30	Impulse-Control Disorder NOS (272)

Adjustment Disorders (273)

309.xx	Adjustment Disorder (273)
.0	With Depressed Mood
.24	With Anxiety
.28	With Mixed Anxiety and Depressed Mood
.3	With Disturbance of Conduct

.4   With Mixed Disturbance of Emotions and
            Conduct
.9   Unspecified
            Specify if: Acute/Chronic

Personality Disorders (275)

Note: *These are coded on Axis II.*
301.0   Paranoid Personality Disorder (276)
301.20   Schizoid Personality Disorder (277)
301.22   Schizotypal Personality Disorder (278)
301.7   Antisocial Personality Disorder (279)
301.83   Borderline Personality Disorder (280)
301.50   Histrionic Personality Disorder (281)
301.81   Narcissistic Personality Disorder (282)
301.82   Avoidant Personality Disorder (283)
301.6   Dependent Personality Disorder (284)
301.4   Obsessive-Compulsive Personality Disorder (285)
301.9   Personality Disorder NOS (286)

Other Conditions That May Be a Focus of Clinical Attention (287)

PSYCHOLOGICAL FACTORS AFFECTING MEDICAL CONDITION (288)
316   . . . *[Specified Psychological Factor]* Affecting . . .
           [Indicate the General Medical Condition] (288)
           Choose name based on nature of factors:
           Mental Disorder Affecting Medical Condition
           Psychological Symptoms Affecting Medical
               Condition
           Personality Traits or Coping Style Affecting
               Medical Condition

Maladaptive Health Behaviors Affecting Medical
Condition
Stress-Related Physiological Response Affecting
Medical Condition
Other or Unspecified Psychological Factors
Affecting Medical Condition

MEDICATION-INDUCED MOVEMENT DISORDERS (289)

332.1   Neuroleptic-Induced Parkinsonism (290)
333.92   Neuroleptic Malignant Syndrome (290)
333.7   Neuroleptic-Induced Acute Dystonia (290)
333.99   Neuroleptic-Induced Acute Akathisia (291)
333.82   Neuroleptic-Induced Tardive Dyskinesia (291)
333.1   Medication-Induced Postural Tremor (291)
333.90   Medication-Induced Movement Disorder
         NOS (292)

OTHER MEDICATION-INDUCED DISORDER (292)

995.2   Adverse Effects of Medication NOS (292)

RELATIONAL PROBLEMS (292)

V61.9   Relational Problem Related to a Mental Disorder
         or General Medical Condition (293)
V61.20   Parent-Child Relational Problem (293)
V61.10   Partner Relational Problem (294)
V61.8   Sibling Relational Problem (294)
V62.81   Relational Problem NOS (294)

PROBLEMS RELATED TO ABUSE OR NEGLECT (294)

V61.21   Physical Abuse of Child (295)
         (code 995.54 if focus of attention is on victim)
V61.21   Sexual Abuse of Child (295)
         (code 995.53 if focus of attention is on victim)
V61.21   Neglect of Child (295)
         (code 995.52 if focus of attention is on victim)

——.——   Physical Abuse of Adult (296)
V61.12   (if by partner)
V62.83   (if by person other than partner)
                  (code 995.81 if focus of attention is on victim)
——.——   Sexual Abuse of Adult (296)
V61.12   (if by partner)
V62.83   (if by person other than partner)
                  (code 995.83 if focus of attention is on victim)

**ADDITIONAL CONDITIONS THAT MAY BE A FOCUS
OF CLINICAL ATTENTION** (296)

V15.81   Noncompliance With Treatment (296)
V65.2   Malingering (297)
V71.01   Adult Antisocial Behavior (298)
V71.02   Child or Adolescent Antisocial Behavior (298)
V62.89   Borderline Intellectual Functioning (298)
              Note: *This is coded on Axis II.*
780.9   Age-Related Cognitive Decline (299)
V62.82   Bereavement (299)
V62.3   Academic Problem (300)
V62.2   Occupational Problem (300)
313.82   Identity Problem (301)
V62.89   Religious or Spiritual Problem (301)
V62.4   Acculturation Problem (301)
V62.89   Phase of Life Problem (301)

Additional Codes

300.9   Unspecified Mental Disorder (nonpsychotic) (303)
V71.09   No Diagnosis or Condition on Axis I (303)
799.9   Diagnosis or Condition Deferred on Axis I (303)
V71.09   No Diagnosis on Axis II (304)
799.9   Diagnosis Deferred on Axis II (304)

Multiaxial System

Axis I	Clinical Disorders Other Conditions That May Be a Focus of Clinical Attention
Axis II	Personality Disorders Mental Retardation
Axis III	General Medical Conditions
Axis IV	Psychosocial and Environmental Problems
Axis V	Global Assessment of Functioning

Multiaxial Assessment

A multiaxial system involves an assessment on several axes, each of which refers to a different domain of information that may help the clinician plan treatment and predict outcome. There are five axes included in the DSM-IV multiaxial classification:

Axis I	Clinical Disorders
	Other Conditions That May Be a Focus of Clinical Attention
Axis II	Personality Disorders
	Mental Retardation
Axis III	General Medical Conditions
Axis IV	Psychosocial and Environmental Problems
Axis V	Global Assessment of Functioning

The use of the multiaxial system facilitates comprehensive and systematic evaluation with attention to the various mental disorders and general medical conditions, psychosocial and environmental problems, and level of functioning that might be overlooked if the focus were on assessing a single presenting problem. A multiaxial system provides a convenient format for organizing and communicating clinical information, for capturing the complexity of clinical situations, and for describing the heterogeneity of individuals presenting with the same diagnosis. In addition, the multiaxial system promotes the application of the biopsychosocial model in clinical, educational, and research settings.

The rest of this section provides a description of each of the DSM-IV axes. In some settings or situations, clinicians may prefer not to use the multiaxial system. For this reason, guidelines for reporting the results of a DSM-IV assessment without applying the formal multiaxial system are provided at the end of this section.

Axis I: Clinical Disorders
Other Conditions That May Be a Focus of Clinical Attention

Axis I is for reporting all the various disorders or conditions in the Classification except for the Personality Disorders and Mental Retardation (which are reported on Axis II). Also reported on Axis I are Other Conditions That May Be a Focus of Clinical Attention.

When an individual has more than one Axis I disorder, all of these should be reported. If more than one Axis I disorder is present, the principal diagnosis or the reason for visit (see p. 5) should be indicated by listing it first. When an individual has both an Axis I and an Axis II disorder, the principal diagnosis or the reason for visit will be assumed to be on Axis I unless the Axis II diagnosis is followed by the qualifying phrase "(Principal Diagnosis)" or "(Reason for Visit)." If no Axis I disorder is present, this should be coded as V71.09. If an Axis I diagnosis is deferred, pending the gathering of additional information, this should be coded as 799.9.

Axis II: Personality Disorders
Mental Retardation

Axis II is for reporting Personality Disorders and Mental Retardation. It may also be used for noting prominent maladaptive personality features and defense mechanisms.

The listing of Personality Disorders and Mental Retardation on a separate axis ensures that consideration will be given to the possible presence of Personality Disorders and Mental Retardation that might otherwise be overlooked when attention is directed to the usually more florid Axis I disorders. The coding of Personality Disorders on Axis II should not be taken to imply that their pathogenesis or range of appropriate treatment is fundamentally different from that for the disorders coded on Axis I.

In the common situation in which an individual has more than one Axis II diagnosis, all should be reported. When an individual has both an Axis I and an Axis II diagnosis and the Axis II diagnosis is the principal diagnosis or the reason for visit, this should be indicated by adding the qualifying phrase "(Principal Diagnosis)" or "(Reason for Visit)" after the Axis II diagnosis. If no Axis II disorder is present, this should be coded as V71.09. If an Axis II diagnosis is deferred, pending the gathering of additional information, this should be coded as 799.9.

Axis II may also be used to indicate prominent maladaptive personality features that do not meet the threshold for a Personality Disorder (in such instances, no code number should be used). The habitual use of maladaptive defense mechanisms may also be indicated on Axis II.

Axis III: General Medical Conditions

Axis III is for reporting current general medical conditions that are potentially relevant to the understanding or management of the individual's mental disorder. These conditions are classified outside the "Mental Disorders" chapter of ICD-9-CM (and outside Chapter V of ICD-10). (For a detailed listing of general medical conditions including the specific ICD-9-CM codes, refer to Appendix G.)

The multiaxial distinction among Axis I, II, and III disorders does not imply that there are fundamental differences in their conceptualization, that mental disorders are unrelated to physical or biological factors or processes, or that general medical conditions are unrelated to behavioral or psychosocial factors or processes. The purpose of distinguishing general medical conditions is to encourage thoroughness in evaluation and to enhance communication among health care providers.

General medical conditions can be related to mental disorders in a variety of ways. In some cases it is clear that the general medical condition is directly etiological to the development or worsening of mental symptoms and that the mechanism for this effect is physiological. When a mental disorder is judged to be a direct physiological consequence of the general medical condition, a Mental Disorder Due to a General Medical Condition should be diagnosed on Axis I and the general medical condition should be recorded on both Axis I and Axis III. For example, when hypothyroidism is a direct cause of depressive symptoms, the designation on Axis I is 293.83 Mood Disorder Due to Hypothyroidism, With Depressive Features, and the hypothyroidism is listed again and coded on Axis III as 244.9.

In those instances in which the etiological relationship between the general medical condition and the mental symptoms is insufficiently clear to warrant an Axis I diagnosis of Mental Disorder Due to a General Medical Condition, the appropriate mental disorder (e.g., Major Depressive Disorder) should be listed and coded on Axis I; the general medical condition should only be coded on Axis III.

There are other situations in which general medical conditions are recorded on Axis III because of their importance to the overall understanding or treatment of the individual with the mental disorder. An Axis I disorder may be a psychological reaction to an Axis III general medical condition (e.g., the development of 309.0 Adjustment Disorder With Depressed Mood as a reaction to the diagnosis of carcinoma of the breast). Some general medical conditions may not be directly related to the mental disorder but nonetheless have important prognostic or treatment implications (e.g., when the diagnosis on Axis I is 296.2 Major Depressive Disorder and on Axis III is 427.9 arrhythmia, the choice of pharmacotherapy is influenced by the general medical condition; or when a person with diabetes mellitus is admitted to the hospital for an exacerbation of Schizophrenia and insulin management must be monitored).

When an individual has more than one clinically relevant Axis III diagnosis, all should be reported. If no Axis III disorder is present, this should be indicated by the notation "Axis III: None." If an Axis III diagnosis is deferred, pending the gathering of additional information, this should be indicated by the notation "Axis III: Deferred."

Axis IV: Psychosocial and Environmental Problems

Axis IV is for reporting psychosocial and environmental problems that may affect the diagnosis, treatment, and prognosis of mental disorders (Axes I and II). A psychosocial or environmental problem may be a negative life event, an environmental difficulty or deficiency, a familial or other interpersonal stress, an inadequacy of social support or personal resources, or other problem relating to the context in which a person's difficulties have developed. So-called positive stressors, such as job promotion, should be listed only if they constitute or lead to a problem, as when a person has difficulty adapting to the new situation. In addition to playing a role in the initiation or exacerbation of a mental disorder, psychosocial problems may also develop as a consequence of a person's psychopathology or may constitute problems that should be considered in the overall management plan.

When an individual has multiple psychosocial or environmental problems, the clinician may note as many as are judged to be relevant. In general, the clinician should note only those psychosocial and environmental problems that have been present during the year preceding the current evaluation. However, the clinician may choose to note psychosocial and environmental problems occurring prior to the previous year if these clearly contribute to the mental disorder or have become a focus of treatment—for example, previous combat experiences leading to Posttraumatic Stress Disorder.

In practice, most psychosocial and environmental problems will be indicated on Axis IV. However, when a psychosocial or environmental problem is the primary focus of clinical attention, it should also be recorded on Axis I, with a code derived from the section "Other Conditions That May Be a Focus of Clinical Attention" (see p. 287).

For convenience, the problems are grouped together in the following categories:

- **Problems with primary support group**—e.g., death of a family member; health problems in family; disruption of family by separation, divorce, or estrangement; removal from the home; remarriage of parent; sexual or physical abuse; parental overprotection; neglect of child; inadequate discipline; discord with siblings; birth of a sibling

- **Problems related to the social environment**—e.g., death or loss of friend; inadequate social support; living alone; difficulty with acculturation; discrimination; adjustment to life-cycle transition (such as retirement)
- **Educational problems**—e.g., illiteracy; academic problems; discord with teachers or classmates; inadequate school environment
- **Occupational problems**—e.g., unemployment; threat of job loss; stressful work schedule; difficult work conditions; job dissatisfaction; job change; discord with boss or co-workers
- **Housing problems**—e.g., homelessness; inadequate housing; unsafe neighborhood; discord with neighbors or landlord
- **Economic problems**—e.g., extreme poverty; inadequate finances; insufficient welfare support
- **Problems with access to health care services**—e.g., inadequate health care services; transportation to health care facilities unavailable; inadequate health insurance
- **Problems related to interaction with the legal system/crime**—e.g., arrest; incarceration; litigation; victim of crime
- **Other psychosocial and environmental problems**—e.g., exposure to disasters, war, other hostilities; discord with nonfamily caregivers such as counselor, social worker, or physician; unavailability of social service agencies

Axis V: Global Assessment of Functioning

Axis V is for reporting the clinician's judgment of the individual's overall level of functioning. This information is useful in planning treatment and measuring its impact, and in predicting outcome.

The reporting of overall functioning on Axis V is done using the Global Assessment of Functioning (GAF) Scale.[1] The GAF Scale may be particularly useful in tracking the clinical progress of individuals in global terms, using a single measure. The GAF Scale is to be rated with respect only to psychological, social, and occupational functioning. The instructions specify, "Do not include impairment in functioning due to physical (or environmental) limitations." In most instances, ratings on the GAF Scale should be for the current period (i.e., the level of functioning at the time of the evaluation) because ratings of current functioning will generally reflect the need for treatment or care. In some settings, it may be useful to note the GAF Scale rating both at time of admission and at time of discharge. The GAF Scale may also be rated for other time periods (e.g., the highest level of functioning for at least a few months during the past

---

[1] The rating of overall psychological functioning on a scale of 0–100 was operationalized by Luborsky in the Health-Sickness Rating Scale (Luborsky L: "Clinicians' Judgments of Mental Health." *Archives of General Psychiatry* 7:407–417, 1962). Spitzer and colleagues developed a revision of the Health-Sickness Rating Scale called the Global Assessment Scale (GAS) (Endicott J, Spitzer RL, Fleiss JL, Cohen J: "The Global Assessment Scale: A Procedure for Measuring Overall Severity of Psychiatric Disturbance." *Archives of General Psychiatry* 33:766–771, 1976). A modified version of the GAS was included in DSM-III-R as the Global Assessment of Functioning (GAF) Scale.

year). The GAF Scale is reported on Axis V as follows: "GAF = ," followed by the GAF rating from 1 to 100, followed by the time period reflected in the rating in parentheses—for example, "(current)," "(highest level in past year)," "(at discharge)."

Global Assessment of Functioning (GAF) Scale

Consider psychological, social, and occupational functioning on a hypothetical continuum of mental health–illness. Do not include impairment in functioning due to physical (or environmental) limitations.

Code (**Note:** Use intermediate codes when appropriate, e.g., 45, 68, 72.)

100 | 91	**Superior functioning in a wide range of activities, life's problems never seem to get out of hand, is sought out by others because of his or her many positive qualities. No symptoms.**
90 | 81	**Absent or minimal symptoms** (e.g., mild anxiety before an exam), **good functioning in all areas, interested and involved in a wide range of activities, socially effective, generally satisfied with life, no more than everyday problems or concerns** (e.g., an occasional argument with family members).
80 | 71	**If symptoms are present, they are transient and expectable reactions to psychosocial stressors** (e.g., difficulty concentrating after family argument); **no more than slight impairment in social, occupational, or school functioning** (e.g., temporarily falling behind in schoolwork).
70 | 61	**Some mild symptoms** (e.g., depressed mood and mild insomnia) **OR some difficulty in social, occupational, or school functioning** (e.g., occasional truancy, or theft within the household), **but generally functioning pretty well, has some meaningful interpersonal relationships.**

60 – 51	**Moderate symptoms** (e.g., flat affect and circumstantial speech, occasional panic attacks) **OR moderate difficulty in social, occupational, or school functioning** (e.g., few friends, conflicts with peers or co-workers).
50 – 41	**Serious symptoms** (e.g., suicidal ideation, severe obsessional rituals, frequent shoplifting) **OR any serious impairment in social, occupational, or school functioning** (e.g., no friends, unable to keep a job).
40 – 31	**Some impairment in reality testing or communication** (e.g., speech is at times illogical, obscure, or irrelevant) **OR major impairment in several areas, such as work or school, family relations, judgment, thinking, or mood** (e.g., depressed man avoids friends, neglects family, and is unable to work; child frequently beats up younger children, is defiant at home, and is failing at school).
30 – 21	**Behavior is considerably influenced by delusions or hallucinations OR serious impairment in communication or judgment** (e.g., sometimes incoherent, acts grossly inappropriately, suicidal preoccupation) **OR inability to function in almost all areas** (e.g., stays in bed all day; no job, home, or friends).
20 – 11	**Some danger of hurting self or others** (e.g., suicide attempts without clear expectation of death; frequently violent; manic excitement) **OR occasionally fails to maintain minimal personal hygiene** (e.g., smears feces) **OR gross impairment in communication** (e.g., largely incoherent or mute).
10 – 1	**Persistent danger of severely hurting self or others** (e.g., recurrent violence) **OR persistent inability to maintain minimal personal hygiene OR serious suicidal act with clear expectation of death.**
0	Inadequate information.

Nonaxial Format

Clinicians who do not wish to use the multiaxial format may simply list the appropriate diagnoses. Those choosing this option should follow the general rule of recording as many coexisting mental disorders, general medical conditions, and other factors as are relevant to the care and treatment of the individual. The Principal Diagnosis or the Reason for Visit should be listed first.

Disorders Usually First Diagnosed in Infancy, Childhood, or Adolescence

This section is devoted to disorders usually first diagnosed in infancy, childhood, or adolescence. This division of the Classification according to age at presentation is for convenience only and is not absolute. Although disorders in this section are usually first evident in childhood and adolescence, some individuals diagnosed with disorders located in this section (e.g., Attention-Deficit/Hyperactivity Disorder) may not present for clinical attention until adulthood. In addition, it is not uncommon for the age at onset for many disorders placed in other sections to be during childhood or adolescence (e.g., Major Depressive Disorder, Schizophrenia, Generalized Anxiety Disorder). Clinicians who work primarily with children and adolescents should therefore be familiar with the entire manual, and those who work primarily with adults should also be familiar with this section.

Mental Retardation

Note: *This is coded on Axis II.*

■ Mental Retardation

A. Significantly subaverage intellectual functioning: an IQ of approximately 70 or below on an individually administered IQ test (for infants, a clinical judgment of significantly subaverage intellectual functioning).

B. Concurrent deficits or impairments in present adaptive functioning (i.e., the person's effectiveness in meeting the standards expected for his or her age by his or her cultural group) in at least two of the following areas: communication, self-care, home living, social/interpersonal skills, use of community resources, self-direction, functional academic skills, work, leisure, health, and safety.

C. The onset is before age 18 years.

Code based on degree of severity reflecting level of intellectual impairment:

    317   **Mild Mental Retardation:**
            IQ level 50–55 to approximately 70
    318.0 **Moderate Mental Retardation:**
            IQ level 35–40 to 50–55
    318.1 **Severe Mental Retardation:**
            IQ level 20–25 to 35–40
    318.2 **Profound Mental Retardation:**
            IQ level below 20 or 25

319   Mental Retardation, Severity Unspecified:
when there is strong presumption of Mental
Retardation but the person's intelligence is
untestable by standard tests (e.g., for individuals
too impaired or uncooperative, or with infants)

Learning Disorders
(*formerly* Academic Skills Disorders)

■ 315.00 Reading Disorder

A. Reading achievement, as measured by individually administered standardized tests of reading accuracy or
comprehension, is substantially below that expected
given the person's chronological age, measured intelligence, and age-appropriate education.

B. The disturbance in Criterion A significantly interferes
with academic achievement or activities of daily living
that require reading skills.

C. If a sensory deficit is present, the reading difficulties are
in excess of those usually associated with it.

Coding note: If a general medical (e.g., neurological) condition
or sensory deficit is present, code the condition on Axis III.

■ 315.1 Mathematics Disorder

A. Mathematical ability, as measured by individually administered standardized tests, is substantially below that
expected given the person's chronological age, measured intelligence, and age-appropriate education.

B. The disturbance in Criterion A significantly interferes with academic achievement or activities of daily living that require mathematical ability.

C. If a sensory deficit is present, the difficulties in mathematical ability are in excess of those usually associated with it.

Coding note: If a general medical (e.g., neurological) condition or sensory deficit is present, code the condition on Axis III.

■ 315.2   Disorder of Written Expression

A. Writing skills, as measured by individually administered standardized tests (or functional assessments of writing skills), are substantially below those expected given the person's chronological age, measured intelligence, and age-appropriate education.

B. The disturbance in Criterion A significantly interferes with academic achievement or activities of daily living that require the composition of written texts (e.g., writing grammatically correct sentences and organized paragraphs).

C. If a sensory deficit is present, the difficulties in writing skills are in excess of those usually associated with it.

Coding note: If a general medical (e.g., neurological) condition or sensory deficit is present, code the condition on Axis III.

■ 315.9   Learning Disorder Not Otherwise Specified

This category is for disorders in learning that do not meet criteria for any specific Learning Disorder. This category might include problems in all three areas (reading, mathematics, written expression) that together significantly interfere with academic achievement even though performance on tests measuring each individual skill is not substantially below that expected given the person's chronological age, measured intelligence, and age-appropriate education.

Motor Skills Disorder

■ 315.4 Developmental Coordination Disorder

A. Performance in daily activities that require motor coordination is substantially below that expected given the person's chronological age and measured intelligence. This may be manifested by marked delays in achieving motor milestones (e.g., walking, crawling, sitting), dropping things, "clumsiness," poor performance in sports, or poor handwriting.

B. The disturbance in Criterion A significantly interferes with academic achievement or activities of daily living.

C. The disturbance is not due to a general medical condition (e.g., cerebral palsy, hemiplegia, or muscular dystrophy) and does not meet criteria for a Pervasive Developmental Disorder.

D. If Mental Retardation is present, the motor difficulties are in excess of those usually associated with it.

Coding note: If a general medical (e.g., neurological) condition or sensory deficit is present, code the condition on Axis III.

Communication Disorders

■ 315.31   Expressive Language Disorder

A. The scores obtained from standardized individually administered measures of expressive language development are substantially below those obtained from standardized measures of both nonverbal intellectual capacity and receptive language development. The disturbance may be manifest clinically by symptoms that include having a markedly limited vocabulary, making errors in tense, or having difficulty recalling words or producing sentences with developmentally appropriate length or complexity.

B. The difficulties with expressive language interfere with academic or occupational achievement or with social communication.

C. Criteria are not met for Mixed Receptive-Expressive Language Disorder or a Pervasive Developmental Disorder.

D. If Mental Retardation, a speech-motor or sensory deficit, or environmental deprivation is present, the language difficulties are in excess of those usually associated with these problems.

Coding note: If a speech-motor or sensory deficit or a neurological condition is present, code the condition on Axis III.

■ 315.32 Mixed Receptive-Expressive Language Disorder

A. The scores obtained from a battery of standardized individually administered measures of both receptive and expressive language development are substantially below those obtained from standardized measures of nonverbal intellectual capacity. Symptoms include those for Expressive Language Disorder as well as difficulty understanding words, sentences, or specific types of words, such as spatial terms.

B. The difficulties with receptive and expressive language significantly interfere with academic or occupational achievement or with social communication.

C. Criteria are not met for a Pervasive Developmental Disorder.

D. If Mental Retardation, a speech-motor or sensory deficit, or environmental deprivation is present, the language difficulties are in excess of those usually associated with these problems.

Coding note: If a speech-motor or sensory deficit or a neurological condition is present, code the condition on Axis III.

■ 315.39 Phonological Disorder (*formerly* Developmental Articulation Disorder)

A. Failure to use developmentally expected speech sounds that are appropriate for age and dialect (e.g., errors in sound production, use, representation, or organization such as, but not limited to, substitutions of one sound for another [use of /t/ for target /k/ sound] or omissions of sounds such as final consonants).

B. The difficulties in speech sound production interfere with academic or occupational achievement or with social communication.

C. If Mental Retardation, a speech-motor or sensory deficit, or environmental deprivation is present, the speech difficulties are in excess of those usually associated with these problems.

Coding note: If a speech-motor or sensory deficit or a neurological condition is present, code the condition on Axis III.

■ 307.0   Stuttering

A. Disturbance in the normal fluency and time patterning of speech (inappropriate for the individual's age), characterized by frequent occurrences of one or more of the following:

  (1)   sound and syllable repetitions
  (2)   sound prolongations
  (3)   interjections
  (4)   broken words (e.g., pauses within a word)
  (5)   audible or silent blocking (filled or unfilled pauses in speech)
  (6)   circumlocutions (word substitutions to avoid problematic words)
  (7)   words produced with an excess of physical tension
  (8)   monosyllabic whole-word repetitions (e.g., "I-I-I-I see him")

B. The disturbance in fluency interferes with academic or occupational achievement or with social communication.

C. If a speech-motor or sensory deficit is present, the speech difficulties are in excess of those usually associated with these problems.

Coding note: If a speech-motor or sensory deficit or a neurological condition is present, code the condition on Axis III.

■ 307.9 Communication Disorder Not Otherwise Specified

This category is for disorders in communication that do not meet criteria for any specific Communication Disorder; for example, a voice disorder (i.e., an abnormality of vocal pitch, loudness, quality, tone, or resonance).

Pervasive Developmental Disorders

■ 299.00 Autistic Disorder

A. A total of six (or more) items from (1), (2), and (3), with at least two from (1), and one each from (2) and (3):

(1) qualitative impairment in social interaction, as manifested by at least two of the following:

(a) marked impairment in the use of multiple nonverbal behaviors such as eye-to-eye gaze, facial expression, body postures, and gestures to regulate social interaction

(b) failure to develop peer relationships appropriate to developmental level

(c) a lack of spontaneous seeking to share enjoyment, interests, or achievements with other people (e.g., by a lack of showing, bringing, or pointing out objects of interest)

(d) lack of social or emotional reciprocity

(2)   qualitative impairments in communication as manifested by at least one of the following:

   (a)   delay in, or total lack of, the development of
         spoken language (not accompanied by an
         attempt to compensate through alternative
         modes of communication such as gesture or
         mime)

   (b)   in individuals with adequate speech, marked
         impairment in the ability to initiate or sustain
         a conversation with others

   (c)   stereotyped and repetitive use of language or
         idiosyncratic language

   (d)   lack of varied, spontaneous make-believe
         play or social imitative play appropriate to
         developmental level

(3)   restricted repetitive and stereotyped patterns of
behavior, interests, and activities, as manifested by
at least one of the following:

   (a)   encompassing preoccupation with one or
         more stereotyped and restricted patterns of
         interest that is abnormal either in intensity or
         focus

   (b)   apparently inflexible adherence to specific,
         nonfunctional routines or rituals

   (c)   stereotyped and repetitive motor mannerisms
         (e.g., hand or finger flapping or twisting, or
         complex whole-body movements)

   (d)   persistent preoccupation with parts of objects

B. Delays or abnormal functioning in at least one of the
following areas, with onset prior to age 3 years: (1) social
interaction, (2) language as used in social communication, or (3) symbolic or imaginative play.

C. The disturbance is not better accounted for by Rett's Disorder or Childhood Disintegrative Disorder.

■ 299.80 Rett's Disorder

A. All of the following:

  (1) apparently normal prenatal and perinatal development

  (2) apparently normal psychomotor development through the first 5 months after birth

  (3) normal head circumference at birth

B. Onset of all of the following after the period of normal development:

  (1) deceleration of head growth between ages 5 and 48 months

  (2) loss of previously acquired purposeful hand skills between ages 5 and 30 months with the subsequent development of stereotyped hand movements (e.g., hand-wringing or hand washing)

  (3) loss of social engagement early in the course (although often social interaction develops later)

  (4) appearance of poorly coordinated gait or trunk movements

  (5) severely impaired expressive and receptive language development with severe psychomotor retardation

■ 299.10 Childhood Disintegrative Disorder

A. Apparently normal development for at least the first 2 years after birth as manifested by the presence of age-appropriate verbal and nonverbal communication, social relationships, play, and adaptive behavior.

B. Clinically significant loss of previously acquired skills (before age 10 years) in at least two of the following areas:

   (1) expressive or receptive language
   (2) social skills or adaptive behavior
   (3) bowel or bladder control
   (4) play
   (5) motor skills

C. Abnormalities of functioning in at least two of the following areas:

   (1) qualitative impairment in social interaction (e.g., impairment in nonverbal behaviors, failure to develop peer relationships, lack of social or emotional reciprocity)
   (2) qualitative impairments in communication (e.g., delay or lack of spoken language, inability to initiate or sustain a conversation, stereotyped and repetitive use of language, lack of varied make-believe play)
   (3) restricted, repetitive, and stereotyped patterns of behavior, interests, and activities, including motor stereotypies and mannerisms

D. The disturbance is not better accounted for by another specific Pervasive Developmental Disorder or by Schizophrenia.

■ 299.80 Asperger's Disorder

A. Qualitative impairment in social interaction, as manifested by at least two of the following:

    (1) marked impairment in the use of multiple nonverbal behaviors such as eye-to-eye gaze, facial expression, body postures, and gestures to regulate social interaction

    (2) failure to develop peer relationships appropriate to developmental level

    (3) a lack of spontaneous seeking to share enjoyment, interests, or achievements with other people (e.g., by a lack of showing, bringing, or pointing out objects of interest to other people)

    (4) lack of social or emotional reciprocity

B. Restricted repetitive and stereotyped patterns of behavior, interests, and activities, as manifested by at least one of the following:

    (1) encompassing preoccupation with one or more stereotyped and restricted patterns of interest that is abnormal either in intensity or focus

    (2) apparently inflexible adherence to specific, nonfunctional routines or rituals

    (3) stereotyped and repetitive motor mannerisms (e.g., hand or finger flapping or twisting, or complex whole-body movements)

    (4) persistent preoccupation with parts of objects

C. The disturbance causes clinically significant impairment in social, occupational, or other important areas of functioning.

D. There is no clinically significant general delay in language (e.g., single words used by age 2 years, communicative phrases used by age 3 years).

E. There is no clinically significant delay in cognitive development or in the development of age-appropriate self-help skills, adaptive behavior (other than in social interaction), and curiosity about the environment in childhood.

F. Criteria are not met for another specific Pervasive Developmental Disorder or Schizophrenia.

■ 299.80 Pervasive Developmental Disorder Not Otherwise Specified (Including Atypical Autism)

This category should be used when there is a severe and pervasive impairment in the development of reciprocal social interaction or verbal and nonverbal communication skills, or when stereotyped behavior, interests, and activities are present, but the criteria are not met for a specific Pervasive Developmental Disorder, Schizophrenia, Schizotypal Personality Disorder, or Avoidant Personality Disorder. For example, this category includes "atypical autism"— presentations that do not meet the criteria for Autistic Disorder because of late age at onset, atypical symptomatology, or subthreshold symptomatology, or all of these.

Attention-Deficit and Disruptive Behavior Disorders

■ Attention-Deficit/Hyperactivity Disorder

A. Either (1) or (2):

   (1)   six (or more) of the following symptoms of **inattention** have persisted for at least 6 months to a degree that is maladaptive and inconsistent with developmental level:

   Inattention
   (a)   often fails to give close attention to details or makes careless mistakes in schoolwork, work, or other activities
   (b)   often has difficulty sustaining attention in tasks or play activities
   (c)   often does not seem to listen when spoken to directly
   (d)   often does not follow through on instructions and fails to finish schoolwork, chores, or duties in the workplace (not due to oppositional behavior or failure to understand instructions)
   (e)   often has difficulty organizing tasks and activities
   (f)   often avoids, dislikes, or is reluctant to engage in tasks that require sustained mental effort (such as schoolwork or homework)
   (g)   often loses things necessary for tasks or activities (e.g., toys, school assignments, pencils, books, or tools)
   (h)   is often easily distracted by extraneous stimuli
   (i)   is often forgetful in daily activities

(2) six (or more) of the following symptoms of **hyperactivity-impulsivity** have persisted for at least 6 months to a degree that is maladaptive and inconsistent with developmental level:

Hyperactivity
(a) often fidgets with hands or feet or squirms in seat
(b) often leaves seat in classroom or in other situations in which remaining seated is expected
(c) often runs about or climbs excessively in situations in which it is inappropriate (in adolescents or adults, may be limited to subjective feelings of restlessness)
(d) often has difficulty playing or engaging in leisure activities quietly
(e) is often "on the go" or often acts as if "driven by a motor"
(f) often talks excessively

Impulsivity
(g) often blurts out answers before questions have been completed
(h) often has difficulty awaiting turn
(i) often interrupts or intrudes on others (e.g., butts into conversations or games)

B. Some hyperactive-impulsive or inattentive symptoms that caused impairment were present before age 7 years.

C. Some impairment from the symptoms is present in two or more settings (e.g., at school [or work] and at home).

D. There must be clear evidence of clinically significant impairment in social, academic, or occupational functioning.

E. The symptoms do not occur exclusively during the course of a Pervasive Developmental Disorder, Schizophrenia, or other Psychotic Disorder and are not better accounted for by another mental disorder (e.g., Mood Disorder, Anxiety Disorder, Dissociative Disorder, or a Personality Disorder).

Code based on type:

314.01 Attention-Deficit/Hyperactivity Disorder, Combined Type: if both Criteria A1 and A2 are met for the past 6 months

314.00 Attention-Deficit/Hyperactivity Disorder, Predominantly Inattentive Type: if Criterion A1 is met but Criterion A2 is not met for the past 6 months

314.01 Attention-Deficit/Hyperactivity Disorder, Predominantly Hyperactive-Impulsive Type: if Criterion A2 is met but Criterion A1 is not met for the past 6 months

Coding note: For individuals (especially adolescents and adults) who currently have symptoms that no longer meet full criteria, "In Partial Remission" should be specified.

■ 314.9 Attention-Deficit/Hyperactivity Disorder Not Otherwise Specified

This category is for disorders with prominent symptoms of inattention or hyperactivity-impulsivity that do not meet criteria for Attention-Deficit/Hyperactivity Disorder.

■ Conduct Disorder

A. A repetitive and persistent pattern of behavior in which the basic rights of others or major age-appropriate societal norms or rules are violated, as manifested by the presence of three (or more) of the following criteria in the past 12 months, with at least one criterion present in the past 6 months:

Aggression to people and animals
(1) often bullies, threatens, or intimidates others
(2) often initiates physical fights
(3) has used a weapon that can cause serious physical harm to others (e.g., a bat, brick, broken bottle, knife, gun)
(4) has been physically cruel to people
(5) has been physically cruel to animals
(6) has stolen while confronting a victim (e.g., mugging, purse snatching, extortion, armed robbery)
(7) has forced someone into sexual activity

Destruction of property
(8) has deliberately engaged in fire setting with the intention of causing serious damage
(9) has deliberately destroyed others' property (other than by fire setting)

Deceitfulness or theft
(10) has broken into someone else's house, building, or car
(11) often lies to obtain goods or favors or to avoid obligations (i.e., "cons" others)
(12) has stolen items of nontrivial value without confronting a victim (e.g., shoplifting, but without breaking and entering; forgery)

Serious violations of rules

(13)   often stays out at night despite parental prohibitions, beginning before age 13 years

(14)   has run away from home overnight at least twice while living in parental or parental surrogate home (or once without returning for a lengthy period)

(15)   often truant from school, beginning before age 13 years

B.   The disturbance in behavior causes clinically significant impairment in social, academic, or occupational functioning.

C.   If the individual is age 18 years or older, criteria are not met for Antisocial Personality Disorder.

Code type based on age at onset:

312.81 Childhood-Onset Type: onset of at least one criterion characteristic of Conduct Disorder prior to age 10 years

312.82 Adolescent-Onset Type: absence of any criteria characteristic of Conduct Disorder prior to age 10 years

312.89 Unspecified Onset: onset of Conduct Disorder is unknown

Specify severity:

Mild: few if any conduct problems in excess of those required to make the diagnosis **and** conduct problems cause only minor harm to others (e.g., lying, truancy, staying out after dark without permission)

Moderate: number of conduct problems and effect on others intermediate between "mild" and "severe" (e.g., stealing without confronting a victim, vandalism)

Severe: many conduct problems in excess of those required to make the diagnosis **or** conduct problems cause considerable harm to others (e.g., forced sex, physical cruelty, use of a weapon, stealing while confronting a victim, breaking and entering)

■ 313.81 Oppositional Defiant Disorder

A. A pattern of negativistic, hostile, and defiant behavior lasting at least 6 months, during which four (or more) of the following are present:

   (1) often loses temper
   (2) often argues with adults
   (3) often actively defies or refuses to comply with adults' requests or rules
   (4) often deliberately annoys people
   (5) often blames others for his or her mistakes or misbehavior
   (6) is often touchy or easily annoyed by others
   (7) is often angry and resentful
   (8) is often spiteful or vindictive

   Note: Consider a criterion met only if the behavior occurs more frequently than is typically observed in individuals of comparable age and developmental level.

B. The disturbance in behavior causes clinically significant impairment in social, academic, or occupational functioning.

C. The behaviors do not occur exclusively during the course of a Psychotic or Mood Disorder.

D. Criteria are not met for Conduct Disorder, and, if the individual is age 18 years or older, criteria are not met for Antisocial Personality Disorder.

■ 312.9   Disruptive Behavior Disorder Not Otherwise Specified

This category is for disorders characterized by conduct or oppositional defiant behaviors that do not meet the criteria for Conduct Disorder or Oppositional Defiant Disorder. For example, include clinical presentations that do not meet full criteria either for Oppositional Defiant Disorder or Conduct Disorder, but in which there is clinically significant impairment.

Feeding and Eating Disorders of Infancy or Early Childhood

■ 307.52   Pica

A. Persistent eating of nonnutritive substances for a period of at least 1 month.

B. The eating of nonnutritive substances is inappropriate to the developmental level.

C. The eating behavior is not part of a culturally sanctioned practice.

D. If the eating behavior occurs exclusively during the course of another mental disorder (e.g., Mental Retardation, Pervasive Developmental Disorder, Schizophrenia), it is sufficiently severe to warrant independent clinical attention.

■ 307.53 Rumination Disorder

A. Repeated regurgitation and rechewing of food for a period of at least 1 month following a period of normal functioning.

B. The behavior is not due to an associated gastrointestinal or other general medical condition (e.g., esophageal reflux).

C. The behavior does not occur exclusively during the course of Anorexia Nervosa or Bulimia Nervosa. If the symptoms occur exclusively during the course of Mental Retardation or a Pervasive Developmental Disorder, they are sufficiently severe to warrant independent clinical attention.

■ 307.59 Feeding Disorder of Infancy or Early Childhood

A. Feeding disturbance as manifested by persistent failure to eat adequately with significant failure to gain weight or significant loss of weight over at least 1 month.

B. The disturbance is not due to an associated gastrointestinal or other general medical condition (e.g., esophageal reflux).

C. The disturbance is not better accounted for by another mental disorder (e.g., Rumination Disorder) or by lack of available food.

D. The onset is before age 6 years.

Tic Disorders

■ 307.23   Tourette's Disorder

A. Both multiple motor and one or more vocal tics have been present at some time during the illness, although not necessarily concurrently. (A *tic* is a sudden, rapid, recurrent, nonrhythmic, stereotyped motor movement or vocalization.)

B. The tics occur many times a day (usually in bouts) nearly every day or intermittently throughout a period of more than 1 year, and during this period there was never a tic-free period of more than 3 consecutive months.

C. The disturbance causes marked distress or significant impairment in social, occupational, or other important areas of functioning.

D. The onset is before age 18 years.

E. The disturbance is not due to the direct physiological effects of a substance (e.g., stimulants) or a general medical condition (e.g., Huntington's disease or post-viral encephalitis).

■ 307.22   Chronic Motor or Vocal Tic Disorder

A. Single or multiple motor or vocal tics (i.e., sudden, rapid, recurrent, nonrhythmic, stereotyped motor movements or vocalizations), but not both, have been present at some time during the illness.

B. The tics occur many times a day nearly every day or intermittently throughout a period of more than 1 year, and during this period there was never a tic-free period of more than 3 consecutive months.

C. The disturbance causes marked distress or significant impairment in social, occupational, or other important areas of functioning.

D. The onset is before age 18 years.

E. The disturbance is not due to the direct physiological effects of a substance (e.g., stimulants) or a general medical condition (e.g., Huntington's disease or post-viral encephalitis).

F. Criteria have never been met for Tourette's Disorder.

■ 307.21   Transient Tic Disorder

A. Single or multiple motor and/or vocal tics (i.e., sudden, rapid, recurrent, nonrhythmic, stereotyped motor movements or vocalizations)

B. The tics occur many times a day, nearly every day for at least 4 weeks, but for no longer than 12 consecutive months.

C. The disturbance causes marked distress or significant impairment in social, occupational, or other important areas of functioning.

D. The onset is before age 18 years.

E. The disturbance is not due to the direct physiological effects of a substance (e.g., stimulants) or a general medical condition (e.g., Huntington's disease or post-viral encephalitis).

F.   Criteria have never been met for Tourette's Disorder or Chronic Motor or Vocal Tic Disorder.

Specify if:
   Single Episode or **Recurrent**

■ 307.20   Tic Disorder Not Otherwise Specified

This category is for disorders characterized by tics that do not meet criteria for a specific Tic Disorder. Examples include tics lasting less than 4 weeks or tics with an onset after age 18 years.

Elimination Disorders

■ Encopresis

A.   Repeated passage of feces into inappropriate places (e.g., clothing or floor) whether involuntary or intentional.

B.   At least one such event a month for at least 3 months.

C.   Chronological age is at least 4 years (or equivalent developmental level).

D.   The behavior is not due exclusively to the direct physiological effects of a substance (e.g., laxatives) or a general medical condition except through a mechanism involving constipation.

Code as follows:

787.6 With Constipation and Overflow Incontinence: there is evidence of constipation on physical examination or by history

307.7 Without Constipation and Overflow Incontinence: there is no evidence of constipation on physical examination or by history

■ 307.6   Enuresis (Not Due to a General Medical Condition)

A. Repeated voiding of urine into bed or clothes (whether involuntary or intentional).

B. The behavior is clinically significant as manifested by either a frequency of twice a week for at least 3 consecutive months or the presence of clinically significant distress or impairment in social, academic (occupational), or other important areas of functioning.

C. Chronological age is at least 5 years (or equivalent developmental level).

D. The behavior is not due exclusively to the direct physiological effect of a substance (e.g., a diuretic) or a general medical condition (e.g., diabetes, spina bifida, a seizure disorder).

Specify type:

Nocturnal Only: passage of urine only during nighttime sleep

Diurnal Only: passage of urine during waking hours

Nocturnal and Diurnal: a combination of the two subtypes above

Other Disorders of Infancy, Childhood, or Adolescence

■ 309.21 Separation Anxiety Disorder

A. Developmentally inappropriate and excessive anxiety concerning separation from home or from those to whom the individual is attached, as evidenced by three (or more) of the following:

   (1) recurrent excessive distress when separation from home or major attachment figures occurs or is anticipated

   (2) persistent and excessive worry about losing, or about possible harm befalling, major attachment figures

   (3) persistent and excessive worry that an untoward event will lead to separation from a major attachment figure (e.g., getting lost or being kidnapped)

   (4) persistent reluctance or refusal to go to school or elsewhere because of fear of separation

   (5) persistently and excessively fearful or reluctant to be alone or without major attachment figures at home or without significant adults in other settings

   (6) persistent reluctance or refusal to go to sleep without being near a major attachment figure or to sleep away from home

   (7) repeated nightmares involving the theme of separation

   (8) repeated complaints of physical symptoms (such as headaches, stomachaches, nausea, or vomiting) when separation from major attachment figures occurs or is anticipated

B. The duration of the disturbance is at least 4 weeks.

C. The onset is before age 18 years.

D. The disturbance causes clinically significant distress or impairment in social, academic (occupational), or other important areas of functioning.

E. The disturbance does not occur exclusively during the course of a Pervasive Developmental Disorder, Schizophrenia, or other Psychotic Disorder and, in adolescents and adults, is not better accounted for by Panic Disorder With Agoraphobia.

Specify if:
   Early Onset: if onset occurs before age 6 years

■ 313.23 Selective Mutism (*formerly* Elective Mutism)

A. Consistent failure to speak in specific social situations (in which there is an expectation for speaking, e.g., at school) despite speaking in other situations.

B. The disturbance interferes with educational or occupational achievement or with social communication.

C. The duration of the disturbance is at least 1 month (not limited to the first month of school).

D. The failure to speak is not due to a lack of knowledge of, or comfort with, the spoken language required in the social situation.

E. The disturbance is not better accounted for by a Communication Disorder (e.g., Stuttering) and does not occur exclusively during the course of a Pervasive Developmental Disorder, Schizophrenia, or other Psychotic Disorder.

■ 313.89   Reactive Attachment Disorder of Infancy or Early Childhood

A. Markedly disturbed and developmentally inappropriate social relatedness in most contexts, beginning before age 5 years, as evidenced by either (1) or (2):

   (1) persistent failure to initiate or respond in a developmentally appropriate fashion to most social interactions, as manifest by excessively inhibited, hypervigilant, or highly ambivalent and contradictory responses (e.g., the child may respond to caregivers with a mixture of approach, avoidance, and resistance to comforting, or may exhibit frozen watchfulness)

   (2) diffuse attachments as manifest by indiscriminate sociability with marked inability to exhibit appropriate selective attachments (e.g., excessive familiarity with relative strangers or lack of selectivity in choice of attachment figures)

B. The disturbance in Criterion A is not accounted for solely by developmental delay (as in Mental Retardation) and does not meet criteria for a Pervasive Developmental Disorder.

C. Pathogenic care as evidenced by at least one of the following:

   (1) persistent disregard of the child's basic emotional needs for comfort, stimulation, and affection

   (2) persistent disregard of the child's basic physical needs

    (3)   repeated changes of primary caregiver that prevent formation of stable attachments (e.g., frequent changes in foster care)

D. There is a presumption that the care in Criterion C is responsible for the disturbed behavior in Criterion A (e.g., the disturbances in Criterion A began following the pathogenic care in Criterion C).

Specify type:
    Inhibited Type: if Criterion A1 predominates in the clinical presentation
    Disinhibited Type: if Criterion A2 predominates in the clinical presentation

■ 307.3 Stereotypic Movement Disorder (*formerly* Stereotypy/Habit Disorder)

A. Repetitive, seemingly driven, and nonfunctional motor behavior (e.g., hand shaking or waving, body rocking, head banging, mouthing of objects, self-biting, picking at skin or bodily orifices, hitting own body).

B. The behavior markedly interferes with normal activities or results in self-inflicted bodily injury that requires medical treatment (or would result in an injury if preventive measures were not used).

C. If Mental Retardation is present, the stereotypic or self-injurious behavior is of sufficient severity to become a focus of treatment.

D. The behavior is not better accounted for by a compulsion (as in Obsessive-Compulsive Disorder), a tic (as in Tic Disorder), a stereotypy that is part of a Pervasive

Developmental Disorder, or hair pulling (as in Trichotillomania).

E. The behavior is not due to the direct physiological effects of a substance or a general medical condition.

F. The behavior persists for 4 weeks or longer.

Specify if:

With Self-Injurious Behavior: if the behavior results in bodily damage that requires specific treatment (or that would result in bodily damage if protective measures were not used)

■ 313.9 Disorder of Infancy, Childhood, or Adolescence Not Otherwise Specified

This category is a residual category for disorders with onset in infancy, childhood, or adolescence that do not meet criteria for any specific disorder in the Classification.

Delirium, Dementia, and Amnestic and Other Cognitive Disorders

Delirium

■ 293.0   Delirium Due to . . . [*Indicate the General Medical Condition*]

A. Disturbance of consciousness (i.e., reduced clarity of awareness of the environment) with reduced ability to focus, sustain, or shift attention.

B. A change in cognition (such as memory deficit, disorientation, language disturbance) or the development of a perceptual disturbance that is not better accounted for by a preexisting, established, or evolving dementia.

C. The disturbance develops over a short period of time (usually hours to days) and tends to fluctuate during the course of the day.

D. There is evidence from the history, physical examination, or laboratory findings that the disturbance is caused by the direct physiological consequences of a general medical condition.

Coding note: If delirium is superimposed on a preexisting Dementia of the Alzheimer's Type or Vascular Dementia, indicate the delirium by coding the appropriate subtype of the dementia, e.g., 290.3 Dementia of the Alzheimer's Type, With Late Onset, With Delirium.

Coding note: Include the name of the general medical condition on Axis I, e.g., 293.0 Delirium Due to Hepatic Encephalopathy; also code the general medical condition on Axis III (see Appendix G for codes).

Substance-Induced Delirium

■ Substance Intoxication Delirium

A. Disturbance of consciousness (i.e., reduced clarity of awareness of the environment) with reduced ability to focus, sustain, or shift attention.

B. A change in cognition (such as memory deficit, disorientation, language disturbance) or the development of a perceptual disturbance that is not better accounted for by a preexisting, established, or evolving dementia.

C. The disturbance develops over a short period of time (usually hours to days) and tends to fluctuate during the course of the day.

D. There is evidence from the history, physical examination, or laboratory findings of either (1) or (2):

   (1) the symptoms in Criteria A and B developed during Substance Intoxication

   (2) medication use is etiologically related to the disturbance[*]

Note: This diagnosis should be made instead of a diagnosis of Substance Intoxication only when the cognitive symptoms are in excess of those usually associated with the intoxication syndrome and when the symptoms are sufficiently severe to warrant independent clinical attention.

*Note: The diagnosis should be recorded as Substance-Induced Delirium if related to medication use. Refer to Appendix G for E-codes indicating specific medications.

Code [Specific Substance] Intoxication Delirium:
(291.0 Alcohol; 292.81 Amphetamine [or Amphetamine-Like Substance]; 292.81 Cannabis; 292.81 Cocaine; 292.81 Hallucinogen; 292.81 Inhalant; 292.81 Opioid; 292.81 Phencyclidine [or Phencyclidine-Like Substance]; 292.81 Sedative, Hypnotic, or Anxiolytic; 292.81 Other [or Unknown] Substance [e.g., cimetidine, digitalis, benztropine])

Coding note: See p. 115 for recording procedures.

■ Substance Withdrawal Delirium

A. Disturbance of consciousness (i.e., reduced clarity of awareness of the environment) with reduced ability to focus, sustain, or shift attention.

B. A change in cognition (such as memory deficit, disorientation, language disturbance) or the development of a perceptual disturbance that is not better accounted for by a preexisting, established, or evolving dementia.

C. The disturbance develops over a short period of time (usually hours to days) and tends to fluctuate during the course of the day.

D. There is evidence from the history, physical examination, or laboratory findings that the symptoms in Criteria A and B developed during, or shortly after, a withdrawal syndrome.

Note: This diagnosis should be made instead of a diagnosis of Substance Withdrawal only when the cognitive symptoms are in excess of those usually associated with the withdrawal syndrome and when the symptoms are sufficiently severe to warrant independent clinical attention.

Code [Specific Substance] Withdrawal Delirium:
(291.0 Alcohol; 292.81 Sedative, Hypnotic, or Anxiolytic; 292.81 Other [or Unknown] Substance)

Coding note: See p. 115 for recording procedures.

■ Delirium Due to Multiple Etiologies

A. Disturbance of consciousness (i.e., reduced clarity of awareness of the environment) with reduced ability to focus, sustain, or shift attention.

B. A change in cognition (such as memory deficit, disorientation, language disturbance) or the development of a perceptual disturbance that is not better accounted for by a preexisting, established, or evolving dementia.

C. The disturbance develops over a short period of time (usually hours to days) and tends to fluctuate during the course of the day.

D. There is evidence from the history, physical examination, or laboratory findings that the delirium has more than one etiology (e.g., more than one etiological general medical condition, a general medical condition plus Substance Intoxication or medication side effect).

Coding note: Delirium Due to Multiple Etiologies does not have its own separate code and should not be recorded as a diagnosis. For example, to code a delirium due to both hepatic encephalopathy and withdrawal from alcohol, the clinician would list both 293.0 Delirium Due to Hepatic Encephalopathy and 291.0 Alcohol Withdrawal Delirium on Axis I and 572.2 hepatic encephalopathy on Axis III.

■ 780.09 Delirium Not Otherwise Specified

This category should be used to diagnose a delirium that does not meet criteria for any of the specific types of delirium described in this section.

Examples include

1. A clinical presentation of delirium that is suspected to be due to a general medical condition or substance use but for which there is insufficient evidence to establish a specific etiology
2. Delirium due to causes not listed in this section (e.g., sensory deprivation)

Dementia

■ Dementia of the Alzheimer's Type

A. The development of multiple cognitive deficits manifested by both

   (1) memory impairment (impaired ability to learn new information or to recall previously learned information)

   (2) one (or more) of the following cognitive disturbances:

      (a) aphasia (language disturbance)

   (b)   apraxia (impaired ability to carry out motor
         activities despite intact motor function)
   (c)   agnosia (failure to recognize or identify ob-
         jects despite intact sensory function)
   (d)   disturbance in executive functioning (i.e.,
         planning, organizing, sequencing, abstracting)

B. The cognitive deficits in Criteria A1 and A2 each cause
    significant impairment in social or occupational func-
    tioning and represent a significant decline from a pre-
    vious level of functioning.

C. The course is characterized by gradual onset and con-
    tinuing cognitive decline.

D. The cognitive deficits in Criteria A1 and A2 are not due
    to any of the following:

    (1)   other central nervous system conditions that cause
          progressive deficits in memory and cognition (e.g.,
          cerebrovascular disease, Parkinson's disease,
          Huntington's disease, subdural hematoma, normal-
          pressure hydrocephalus, brain tumor)
    (2)   systemic conditions that are known to cause de-
          mentia (e.g., hypothyroidism, vitamin B_{12} or folic
          acid deficiency, niacin deficiency, hypercalcemia,
          neurosyphilis, HIV infection)
    (3)   substance-induced conditions

E. The deficits do not occur exclusively during the course
    of a delirium.

F. The disturbance is not better accounted for by another
    Axis I disorder (e.g., Major Depressive Disorder, Schizo-
    phrenia).

Code based on type of onset and predominant features:

With Early Onset: if onset is at age 65 years or below

290.11 With Delirium: if delirium is superimposed on the dementia

290.12 With Delusions: if delusions are the predominant feature

290.13 With Depressed Mood: if depressed mood (including presentations that meet full symptom criteria for a Major Depressive Episode) is the predominant feature. A separate diagnosis of Mood Disorder Due to a General Medical Condition is not given.

290.10 Uncomplicated: if none of the above predominates in the current clinical presentation

With Late Onset: if onset is after age 65 years

290.3 With Delirium: if delirium is superimposed on the dementia

290.20 With Delusions: if delusions are the predominant feature

290.21 With Depressed Mood: if depressed mood (including presentations that meet full symptom criteria for a Major Depressive Episode) is the predominant feature. A separate diagnosis of Mood Disorder Due to a General Medical Condition is not given.

290.0 Uncomplicated: if none of the above predominates in the current clinical presentation

Specify if (can be applied to any of the above subtypes):

With Behavioral Disturbance: if there is clinically significant behavioral disturbance (e.g., wandering)

Coding note: Also code 331.0 Alzheimer's disease on Axis III.

■ 290.4x Vascular Dementia (*formerly Multi-Infarct Dementia*)

A. The development of multiple cognitive deficits manifested by both

(1) memory impairment (impaired ability to learn new information or to recall previously learned information)

(2) one (or more) of the following cognitive disturbances:

(a) aphasia (language disturbance)

(b) apraxia (impaired ability to carry out motor activities despite intact motor function)

(c) agnosia (failure to recognize or identify objects despite intact sensory function)

(d) disturbance in executive functioning (i.e., planning, organizing, sequencing, abstracting)

B. The cognitive deficits in Criteria A1 and A2 each cause significant impairment in social or occupational functioning and represent a significant decline from a previous level of functioning.

C. Focal neurological signs and symptoms (e.g., exaggeration of deep tendon reflexes, extensor plantar response, pseudobulbar palsy, gait abnormalities, weakness of an extremity) or laboratory evidence indicative of cerebrovascular disease (e.g., multiple infarctions involving cortex and underlying white matter) that are judged to be etiologically related to the disturbance.

D. The deficits do not occur exclusively during the course of a delirium.

Code based on predominant features:

290.41 With Delirium: if delirium is superimposed on the dementia

290.42 With Delusions: if delusions are the predominant feature

290.43 With Depressed Mood: if depressed mood (including presentations that meet full symptom criteria for a Major Depressive Episode) is the predominant feature. A separate diagnosis of Mood Disorder Due to a General Medical Condition is not given.

290.40 Uncomplicated: if none of the above predominates in the current clinical presentation

Specify if (can be applied to any of the above subtypes):

With Behavioral Disturbance: if there is clinically significant behavioral disturbance (e.g., wandering)

Coding note: Also code cerebrovascular condition on Axis III.

■ Dementia Due to Other General Medical Conditions

A. The development of multiple cognitive deficits manifested by both

  (1) memory impairment (impaired ability to learn new information or to recall previously learned information)

  (2) one (or more) of the following cognitive disturbances:

   (a) aphasia (language disturbance)

   (b) apraxia (impaired ability to carry out motor activities despite intact motor function)

   (c) agnosia (failure to recognize or identify objects despite intact sensory function)

   (d)   disturbance in executive functioning (i.e., planning, organizing, sequencing, abstracting)

B.   The cognitive deficits in Criteria A1 and A2 each cause significant impairment in social or occupational functioning and represent a significant decline from a previous level of functioning.

C.   There is evidence from the history, physical examination, or laboratory findings that the disturbance is the direct physiological consequence of one of the general medical conditions listed below.

D.   The deficits do not occur exclusively during the course of a delirium.

Code based on etiological general medical condition:

294.1   Dementia Due to HIV Disease   *Coding note:* Also code 042 HIV infection affecting central nervous system on Axis III.

294.1   Dementia Due to Head Trauma   *Coding note:* Also code 854.00 head injury on Axis III.

294.1   Dementia Due to Parkinson's Disease   *Coding note:* Also code 332.0 Parkinson's disease on Axis III.

294.1   Dementia Due to Huntington's Disease   *Coding note:* Also code 333.4 Huntington's disease on Axis III.

290.10   Dementia Due to Pick's Disease   *Coding note:* Also code 331.1 Pick's disease on Axis III.

290.10   Dementia Due to Creutzfeldt-Jakob Disease   *Coding note:* Also code 046.1 Creutzfeldt-Jakob disease on Axis III.

294.1   Dementia Due to . . . [Indicate the General Medical Condition not listed above] (e.g., normal-pressure hydrocephalus, hypothyroidism, brain tumor, vitamin B$_{12}$ deficiency, intracranial radiation) *Coding note:* Also code the etiological general medical condition on Axis III. See Appendix G for selected ICD-9-CM diagnostic codes.

■ Substance-Induced Persisting Dementia

A. The development of multiple cognitive deficits manifested by both

   (1) memory impairment (impaired ability to learn new information or to recall previously learned information)

   (2) one (or more) of the following cognitive disturbances:

      (a) aphasia (language disturbance)

      (b) apraxia (impaired ability to carry out motor activities despite intact motor function)

      (c) agnosia (failure to recognize or identify objects despite intact sensory function)

      (d) disturbance in executive functioning (i.e., planning, organizing, sequencing, abstracting)

B. The cognitive deficits in Criteria A1 and A2 each cause significant impairment in social or occupational functioning and represent a significant decline from a previous level of functioning.

C. The deficits do not occur exclusively during the course of a delirium and persist beyond the usual duration of Substance Intoxication or Withdrawal.

D. There is evidence from the history, physical examination, or laboratory findings that the deficits are etiologically related to the persisting effects of substance use (e.g., a drug of abuse, a medication).

Code [Specific Substance]–Induced Persisting Dementia: (291.2 Alcohol; 292.82 Inhalant; 292.82 Sedative, Hypnotic, or Anxiolytic; 292.82 Other [or Unknown] Substance)

Coding note: See p. 115 for recording procedures.

■ Dementia Due to Multiple Etiologies

A. The development of multiple cognitive deficits manifested by both

   (1) memory impairment (impaired ability to learn new information or to recall previously learned information)
   (2) one (or more) of the following cognitive disturbances:

      (a) aphasia (language disturbance)
      (b) apraxia (impaired ability to carry out motor activities despite intact motor function)
      (c) agnosia (failure to recognize or identify objects despite intact sensory function)
      (d) disturbance in executive functioning (i.e., planning, organizing, sequencing, abstracting)

B. The cognitive deficits in Criteria A1 and A2 each cause significant impairment in social or occupational functioning and represent a significant decline from a previous level of functioning.

C. There is evidence from the history, physical examination, or laboratory findings that the disturbance has more than one etiology (e.g., head trauma plus chronic alcohol use, Dementia of the Alzheimer's Type with the subsequent development of Vascular Dementia).

D. The deficits do not occur exclusively during the course of a delirium.

Coding note: Dementia Due to Multiple Etiologies does not have its own separate code and should not be recorded as a diagnosis. For example, both Dementia of the Alzheimer's Type and Vascular Dementia should be diagnosed for an individual with Dementia of the Alzheimer's Type, With Late Onset, Uncomplicated, who, over the course of several strokes, develops a significant further decline in cognitive functioning. In this example, the clinician would list both 290.0 Dementia of the Alzheimer's Type, With Late Onset, Uncomplicated, and 290.40, Vascular Dementia, Uncomplicated, on Axis I, and 331.0 Alzheimer's Disease and 436 Stroke on Axis III.

■ 294.8   Dementia Not Otherwise Specified

This category should be used to diagnose a dementia that does not meet criteria for any of the specific types described in this section.

An example is a clinical presentation of dementia for which there is insufficient evidence to establish a specific etiology.

Amnestic Disorders

■ 294.0   Amnestic Disorder Due to . . . [*Indicate the General Medical Condition*]

A. The development of memory impairment as manifested by impairment in the ability to learn new information or the inability to recall previously learned information.

B. The memory disturbance causes significant impairment in social or occupational functioning and represents a significant decline from a previous level of functioning.

C. The memory disturbance does not occur exclusively during the course of a delirium or a dementia.

D. There is evidence from the history, physical examination, or laboratory findings that the disturbance is the direct physiological consequence of a general medical condition (including physical trauma).

Specify if:
> **Transient:** if memory impairment lasts for 1 month or less. When the diagnosis is made within the first month without waiting for recovery, the term "provisional" may be added.
> **Chronic:** if memory impairment lasts for more than 1 month

Coding note: Include the name of the general medical condition on Axis I, e.g., 294.0 Amnestic Disorder Due to Head Trauma; also code the general medical condition on Axis III (see Appendix G for codes).

■ Substance-Induced Persisting Amnestic Disorder

A. The development of memory impairment as manifested by impairment in the ability to learn new information or the inability to recall previously learned information.

B. The memory disturbance causes significant impairment in social or occupational functioning and represents a significant decline from a previous level of functioning.

C. The memory disturbance does not occur exclusively during the course of a delirium or a dementia and persists beyond the usual duration of Substance Intoxication or Withdrawal.

D. There is evidence from the history, physical examination, or laboratory findings that the memory disturbance is etiologically related to the persisting effects of substance use (e.g., a drug of abuse, a medication).

Code [Specific Substance]–Induced Persisting Amnestic Disorder:

(291.1 Alcohol; 292.83 Sedative, Hypnotic, or Anxiolytic; 292.83 Other [or Unknown] Substance)

Coding note: See p. 115 for recording procedures.

■ 294.8 Amnestic Disorder Not Otherwise Specified

This category should be used to diagnose an amnestic disorder that does not meet criteria for any of the specific types described in this section.

An example is a clinical presentation of amnesia for which there is insufficient evidence to establish a specific etiology (i.e., dissociative, substance induced, or due to a general medical condition).

Other Cognitive Disorders

294.9 Cognitive Disorder
Not Otherwise Specified

This category is for disorders that are characterized by cognitive dysfunction presumed to be due to the direct physiological effect of a general medical condition that do not meet criteria for any of the specific deliriums, dementias, or amnestic disorders listed in this section and that are not better classified as Delirium Not Otherwise Specified, Dementia Not Otherwise Specified, or Amnestic Disorder Not Otherwise Specified. For cognitive dysfunction due to a specific or unknown substance, the specific Substance-Related Disorder Not Otherwise Specified category should be used.

Examples include

1. Mild neurocognitive disorder: impairment in cognitive functioning as evidenced by neuropsychological testing or quantified clinical assessment, accompanied by objective evidence of a systemic general medical condition or central nervous system dysfunction (see Appendix B in DSM-IV for suggested research criteria)
2. Postconcussional disorder: following a head trauma, impairment in memory or attention with associated symptoms (see Appendix B in DSM-IV for suggested research criteria)

Mental Disorders Due to a General Medical Condition

A Mental Disorder Due to a General Medical Condition is characterized by the presence of mental symptoms that are judged to be the direct physiological consequence of a general medical condition. The term *general medical condition* refers to conditions that are coded on Axis III and that are listed outside the "Mental Disorders" chapter of ICD. (See Appendix G for a condensed list of these conditions.) Maintaining the distinction between mental disorders and general medical conditions does not imply that there are fundamental differences in their conceptualization, that mental disorders are unrelated to physical or biological factors or processes, or that general medical conditions are unrelated to behavioral or psychosocial factors or processes. The purpose of distinguishing general medical conditions from mental disorders is to encourage thoroughness in evaluation and to provide a shorthand term to enhance communication among health care providers. However, in clinical practice, it is expected that more specific terminology will be used to identify the specific condition involved.

Criteria sets for three of these disorders (i.e., Catatonic Disorder Due to a General Medical Condition, Personality Change Due to a General Medical Condition, and Mental Disorder Not Otherwise Specified Due to a General Medical Condition) are included in this section. The criteria for the conditions listed below are placed in other sections of the manual with disorders with which they share phenomenology. The manual has been organized in this fashion to alert clinicians to consider these disorders in making a differential diagnosis.

■ 293.89 Catatonic Disorder Due to . . . [*Indicate the General Medical Condition*]

A. The presence of catatonia as manifested by motoric immobility, excessive motor activity (that is apparently purposeless and not influenced by external stimuli), extreme negativism or mutism, peculiarities of voluntary movement, or echolalia or echopraxia.

B. There is evidence from the history, physical examination, or laboratory findings that the disturbance is the direct physiological consequence of a general medical condition.

C. The disturbance is not better accounted for by another mental disorder (e.g., a Manic Episode).

D. The disturbance does not occur exclusively during the course of a delirium.

Coding note: Include the name of the general medical condition on Axis I, e.g., 293.89 Catatonic Disorder Due to Hepatic Encephalopathy; also code the general medical condition on Axis III (see Appendix G for codes).

■ 310.1 Personality Change Due to . . . [*Indicate the General Medical Condition*]

A. A persistent personality disturbance that represents a change from the individual's previous characteristic personality pattern. (In children, the disturbance involves a marked deviation from normal development or a significant change in the child's usual behavior patterns lasting at least 1 year).

B. There is evidence from the history, physical examination, or laboratory findings that the disturbance is the direct physiological consequence of a general medical condition.

C. The disturbance is not better accounted for by another mental disorder (including other Mental Disorders Due to a General Medical Condition).

D. The disturbance does not occur exclusively during the course of a delirium and does not meet criteria for a dementia.

E. The disturbance causes clinically significant distress or impairment in social, occupational, or other important areas of functioning.

Specify type:

Labile Type: if the predominant feature is affective lability

Disinhibited Type: if the predominant feature is poor impulse control as evidenced by sexual indiscretions, etc.

Aggressive Type: if the predominant feature is aggressive behavior

Apathetic Type: if the predominant feature is marked apathy and indifference

Paranoid Type: if the predominant feature is suspiciousness or paranoid ideation

Other Type: if the predominant feature is not one of the above, e.g., personality change associated with a seizure disorder

Combined Type: if more than one feature predominates in the clinical picture

Unspecified Type

Coding note: Include the name of the general medical condition on Axis I, e.g., 310.1 Personality Change Due to Temporal Lobe Epilepsy; also code the general medical condition on Axis III (see Appendix G for codes).

■ 293.9   Mental Disorder Not Otherwise Specified Due to a General Medical Condition

This residual category should be used for situations in which it has been established that the disturbance is caused by the direct physiological effects of a general medical condition, but the criteria are not met for a specific Mental Disorder Due to a General Medical Condition (e.g., dissociative symptoms due to complex partial seizures).

Coding note: Include the name of the general medical condition on Axis I, e.g., 293.9 Mental Disorder Not Otherwise Specified Due to HIV Disease; also code the general medical condition on Axis III (see Appendix G for codes).

Substance-Related Disorders

The Substance-Related Disorders are divided into two groups: the Substance Use Disorders (Substance Dependence and Substance Abuse) and the Substance-Induced Disorders (Substance Intoxication, Substance Withdrawal, Substance-Induced Delirium, Substance-Induced Persisting Dementia, Substance-Induced Persisting Amnestic Disorder, Substance-Induced Psychotic Disorder, Substance-Induced Mood Disorder, Substance-Induced Anxiety Disorder, Substance-Induced Sexual Dysfunction, and Substance-Induced Sleep Disorder). The section begins with the criteria sets for Substance Dependence, Abuse, Intoxication, and Withdrawal that are applicable across classes of substances. Table 1 indicates which specific classes of substances have a defined Dependence, Abuse, Intoxication, or Withdrawal syndrome. The remainder of the section is organized by class of substance and includes criteria sets for substance-specific Intoxication and Withdrawal for each of the 11 classes of substances. To facilitate differential diagnosis, criteria for the remaining Substance-Induced Disorders are included in the sections of the manual with disorders with which they share phenomenology:

Substance-Induced Delirium (see p. 82) is included in the "Delirium, Dementia, and Amnestic and Other Cognitive Disorders" section.

Substance-Induced Persisting Dementia (see p. 91) is included in the "Delirium, Dementia, and Amnestic and Other Cognitive Disorders" section.

Substance-Induced Persisting Amnestic Disorder (see p. 94) is included in the "Delirium, Dementia, and Amnestic and Other Cognitive Disorders" section.

Substance-Induced Psychotic Disorder (see p. 157) is included in the "Schizophrenia and Other Psychotic Disorders" section. (In DSM-III-R these disorders were classified as "organic hallucinosis" and "organic delusional disorder.")

Substance-Induced Mood Disorder (see p. 184) is included in the "Mood Disorders" section.

Substance-Induced Anxiety Disorder (see p. 215) is included in the "Anxiety Disorders" section.

Substance-Induced Sexual Dysfunction (see p. 240) is included in the "Sexual and Gender Identity Disorders" section.

Substance-Induced Sleep Disorder (see p. 266) is included in the "Sleep Disorders" section.

In addition, **Hallucinogen Persisting Perception Disorder (Flashbacks)** (p. 130) is included under "Hallucinogen-Related Disorders" in this section.

The substance-induced diagnoses associated with each specific class of substances that are placed in other sections of the Classification are shown in Table 2.

Table 1. Diagnoses associated with class of substances

	Dependence	Abuse	Intoxication	Withdrawal
Alcohol	X	X	X	X
Amphetamines	X	X	X	X
Caffeine			X	
Cannabis	X	X	X	
Cocaine	X	X	X	X
Hallucinogens	X	X	X	
Inhalants	X	X	X	
Nicotine	X			X
Opioids	X	X	X	X
Phencyclidine	X	X	X	
Sedatives, hypnotics, or anxiolytics	X	X	X	X
Polysubstance	X			
Other	X	X	X	X

Note: X indicates that the category is recognized in DSM-IV.

Table 2. Substance-Induced Disorders associated with class of substances

	Intoxi-cation Delirium	With-drawal Delirium	Dementia	Amnestic Disorder	Psychotic Disorders
Alcohol	I	W	P	P	I/W
Amphetamines	I				I
Caffeine					
Cannabis	I				I
Cocaine	I				I
Hallucinogens	I				I*
Inhalants	I		P		I
Nicotine					
Opioids	I				I
Phencyclidine	I				I
Sedatives, hypnotics, or anxiolytics	I	W	P	P	I/W
Other	I	W	P	P	I/W

*Also Hallucinogen Persisting Perception Disorder (Flashbacks).
Note: I, W, I/W, or P indicates that the category is recognized in DSM-IV. In addition, *I* indicates that the specifier With Onset During Intoxication may be noted for the category (except for Intoxication Delirium); *W* indicates that the specifier With Onset During Withdrawal may be noted for the category (except for Withdrawal Delirium); and *I/W* indicates that either With Onset During Intoxication or With Onset During Withdrawal may be noted for the category. *P* indicates that the disorder is Persisting.

Mood Disorders	Anxiety Disorders	Sexual Dysfunctions	Sleep Disorders
I/W	I/W	I	I/W
I/W	I	I	I/W
	I		I
	I		
I/W	I/W	I	I/W
I	I		
I	I		
I		I	I/W
I	I		
I/W	W	I	I/W
I/W	I/W	I	I/W

Substance Use Disorders

■ Substance Dependence

A maladaptive pattern of substance use, leading to clinically significant impairment or distress, as manifested by three (or more) of the following, occurring at any time in the same 12-month period:

(1) tolerance, as defined by either of the following:

   (a) a need for markedly increased amounts of the substance to achieve intoxication or desired effect

   (b) markedly diminished effect with continued use of the same amount of the substance

(2) withdrawal, as manifested by either of the following:

   (a) the characteristic withdrawal syndrome for the substance (refer to Criteria A and B of the criteria sets for Withdrawal from the specific substances)

   (b) the same (or a closely related) substance is taken to relieve or avoid withdrawal symptoms

(3) the substance is often taken in larger amounts or over a longer period than was intended

(4) there is a persistent desire or unsuccessful efforts to cut down or control substance use

(5) a great deal of time is spent in activities necessary to obtain the substance (e.g., visiting multiple doctors or driving long distances), use the substance (e.g., chain-smoking), or recover from its effects

   (6)   important social, occupational, or recreational activities are given up or reduced because of substance use

   (7)   the substance use is continued despite knowledge of having a persistent or recurrent physical or psychological problem that is likely to have been caused or exacerbated by the substance (e.g., current cocaine use despite recognition of cocaine-induced depression, or continued drinking despite recognition that an ulcer was made worse by alcohol consumption)

Specify if:

    With Physiological Dependence: evidence of tolerance or withdrawal (i.e., either Item 1 or 2 is present)

    Without Physiological Dependence: no evidence of tolerance or withdrawal (i.e., neither Item 1 nor 2 is present)

Course Specifiers

Six course specifiers are available for Substance Dependence. The four Remission specifiers can be applied only after none of the criteria for Substance Dependence or Substance Abuse have been present for at least 1 month. The definition of these four types of Remission is based on the interval of time that has elapsed since the cessation of Dependence (Early versus Sustained Remission) and whether there is continued presence of one or more of the items included in the criteria sets for Dependence or Abuse (Partial versus Full Remission). Because the first 12 months following Dependence is a time of particularly high risk for relapse, this period is designated Early Remission. After 12 months of Early Remission have passed without relapse to Dependence, the person enters into Sustained Remission. For both Early Remission and Sustained Remission, a further designation of Full is given if no criteria for Dependence or Abuse have been met during the period of remission; a designation of Partial is given if at least one of the criteria for Dependence or Abuse has been met, intermittently or continuously, during the period of remission. The differentiation of Sustained Full Remission from recovered (no current Substance Use Disorder) requires consideration of the length of time since the last period of disturbance, the total duration of the disturbance, and the need for continued evaluation. If, after a period of remission or recovery, the individual again becomes dependent, the application of the Early Remission specifier requires that there again be at least 1 month in which no criteria for Dependence or Abuse are met. Two additional specifiers have been provided: On Agonist Therapy and In a Controlled Environment. For an individual to qualify for Early Remission after cessation of agonist therapy or release from a controlled environment, there must be a 1-month period in which none of the criteria for Dependence or Abuse are met.

The following Remission specifiers can be applied only after no criteria for Dependence or Abuse have been met for at least 1 month. Note that these specifiers do not apply if the individual is on agonist therapy or in a controlled environment (see below).

Early Full Remission.   This specifier is used if, for at least 1 month, but for less than 12 months, no criteria for Dependence or Abuse have been met.

⊢– Dependence –⊪– 1   –⊪–0–11 months ─────────⊣
                 month

Early Partial Remission. This specifier is used if, for at least 1 month, but less than 12 months, one or more criteria for Dependence or Abuse have been met (but the full criteria for Dependence have not been met).

Dependence — 1 month — 0–11 months

Sustained Full Remission. This specifier is used if none of the criteria for Dependence or Abuse have been met at any time during a period of 12 months or longer.

Dependence — 1 month — 11+ months

Sustained Partial Remission. This specifier is used if full criteria for Dependence have not been met for a period of 12 months or longer; however, one or more criteria for Dependence or Abuse have been met.

Dependence — 1 month — 11+ months

The following specifiers apply if the individual is on agonist therapy or in a controlled environment:

On Agonist Therapy. This specifier is used if the individual is on a prescribed agonist medication, and no criteria for Dependence or Abuse have been met for that class of medication for at least the past month (except tolerance to, or withdrawal from, the agonist). This category also applies to those being treated for Dependence using a partial agonist or an agonist/antagonist.

In a Controlled Environment. This specifier is used if the individual is in an environment where access to alcohol and controlled substances is restricted, and no criteria for Dependence or Abuse have been met for at least the past month. Examples of these environments are closely supervised and substance-free jails, therapeutic communities, or locked hospital units.

■ Substance Abuse

A. A maladaptive pattern of substance use leading to clinically significant impairment or distress, as manifested by one (or more) of the following, occurring within a 12-month period:

  (1) recurrent substance use resulting in a failure to fulfill major role obligations at work, school, or home (e.g., repeated absences or poor work performance related to substance use; substance-related absences, suspensions, or expulsions from school; neglect of children or household)

  (2) recurrent substance use in situations in which it is physically hazardous (e.g., driving an automobile or operating a machine when impaired by substance use)

  (3) recurrent substance-related legal problems (e.g., arrests for substance-related disorderly conduct)

  (4) continued substance use despite having persistent or recurrent social or interpersonal problems caused or exacerbated by the effects of the substance (e.g., arguments with spouse about consequences of intoxication, physical fights)

B. The symptoms have never met the criteria for Substance Dependence for this class of substance.

Substance-Induced Disorders

■ Substance Intoxication

A. The development of a reversible substance-specific syndrome due to recent ingestion of (or exposure to) a substance. **Note:** Different substances may produce similar or identical syndromes.

B. Clinically significant maladaptive behavioral or psychological changes that are due to the effect of the substance on the central nervous system (e.g., belligerence, mood lability, cognitive impairment, impaired judgment, impaired social or occupational functioning) and develop during or shortly after use of the substance.

C. The symptoms are not due to a general medical condition and are not better accounted for by another mental disorder.

■ Substance Withdrawal

A. The development of a substance-specific syndrome due to the cessation of (or reduction in) substance use that has been heavy and prolonged.

B. The substance-specific syndrome causes clinically significant distress or impairment in social, occupational, or other important areas of functioning.

C. The symptoms are not due to a general medical condition and are not better accounted for by another mental disorder.

Recording Procedures for Dependence, Abuse, Intoxication, and Withdrawal

For drugs of abuse.   The clinician should use the code that applies to the class of substances, but record the name of the specific substance rather than the name of the class. For example, the clinician should record 292.0 Secobarbital Withdrawal (rather than Sedative, Hypnotic, or Anxiolytic Withdrawal) or 305.70 Methamphetamine Abuse (rather than Amphetamine Abuse). For substances that do not fit into any of the classes (e.g., amyl nitrite), the appropriate code for "Other Substance Dependence," "Other Substance Abuse," "Other Substance Intoxication," or "Other Substance Withdrawal" should be used and the specific substance indicated (e.g., 305.90 Amyl Nitrite Abuse). If the substance taken by the individual is unknown, the code for the class "Other (or Unknown)" should be used (e.g., 292.89 Unknown Substance Intoxication). For a particular substance, if criteria are met for more than one Substance-Related Disorder, all should be diagnosed (e.g., 292.0 Heroin Withdrawal; 304.00 Heroin Dependence). If there are symptoms or problems associated with a particular substance but criteria are not met for any of the substance-specific disorders, the Not Otherwise Specified category can be used (e.g., 292.9 Cannabis-Related Disorder Not Otherwise Specified). If multiple substances are used, all relevant Substance-Related Disorders should be diagnosed (e.g., 292.89 Mescaline Intoxication; 304.20 Cocaine Dependence). The situations in which a diagnosis of 304.80 Polysubstance Dependence should be given are described on p. 143.

For medications and toxins.   For medications not covered above (as well as for toxins), the code for "Other Substance" should be used. The specific medication can coded by also listing the appropriate E-code on Axis I (see Appendix G) (e.g., 292.89 Benztropine Intoxication; E941.1 Benztropine). E-codes should also be used for classes of substances listed above when they are taken as prescribed medications (e.g., opioids).

Recording Procedures for Substance-Induced Mental Disorders Included Elsewhere in the Manual

The name of the diagnosis begins with the specific substance (e.g., cocaine, diazepam, dexamethasone) that is presumed to be causing the symptoms. The diagnostic code is selected from the listing of classes of substances provided in the criteria sets for the particular Substance-Induced Disorder. For substances that do not fit into any of the classes (e.g., dexamethasone), the code for "Other Substance" should be used. In addition, for medications prescribed at therapeutic doses, the specific medication can be indicated by listing the appropriate E-code on Axis I (see Appendix G). The name of the disorder (e.g., Cocaine-Induced Psychotic Disorder; Diazepam-Induced Anxiety Disorder) is followed by the specification of the predominant symptom presentation and the context in which the symptoms developed (e.g., 292.11 Cocaine-Induced Psychotic Disorder, With Delusions, With Onset During Intoxication; 292.89 Diazepam-Induced Anxiety Disorder, With Onset During Withdrawal). When more than one substance is judged to play a significant role in the development of symptoms, each should be listed separately. If a substance is judged to be the etiological factor, but the specific substance or class of substances is unknown, the class "Unknown Substance" should be used.

Alcohol-Related Disorders

Alcohol Use Disorders

303.90 Alcohol Dependence (see p. 108 for criteria)
305.00 Alcohol Abuse (see p. 112 for criteria)

Alcohol-Induced Disorders

303.00 Alcohol Intoxication (see below for criteria)
291.81 Alcohol Withdrawal (see below for criteria)
291.0   Alcohol Intoxication Delirium (see p. 82 for criteria)
291.0   Alcohol Withdrawal Delirium (see p. 83 for criteria)
291.2   Alcohol-Induced Persisting Dementia (see p. 91 for criteria)
291.1   Alcohol-Induced Persisting Amnestic Disorder (see p. 94 for criteria)
291.5   Alcohol-Induced Psychotic Disorder, With Delusions (see p. 157 for criteria) *Specify if:* With Onset During Intoxication/With Onset During Withdrawal
291.3   Alcohol-Induced Psychotic Disorder, With Hallucinations (see p. 157 for criteria) *Specify if:* With Onset During Intoxication/With Onset During Withdrawal
291.89 Alcohol-Induced Mood Disorder (see p. 184 for criteria) *Specify if:* With Onset During Intoxication/With Onset During Withdrawal
291.89 Alcohol-Induced Anxiety Disorder (see p. 215 for criteria) *Specify if:* With Onset During Intoxication/With Onset During Withdrawal

291.89   Alcohol-Induced Sexual Dysfunction (see p. 240 for criteria) *Specify if:* With Onset During Intoxication

291.89   Alcohol-Induced Sleep Disorder (see p. 266 for criteria) *Specify if:* With Onset During Intoxication/With Onset During Withdrawal

291.9   Alcohol-Related Disorder Not Otherwise Specified
The Alcohol-Related Disorder Not Otherwise Specified category is for disorders associated with the use of alcohol that are not classifiable as one of the disorders listed above.

■ 303.00 Alcohol Intoxication

A. Recent ingestion of alcohol.

B. Clinically significant maladaptive behavioral or psychological changes (e.g., inappropriate sexual or aggressive behavior, mood lability, impaired judgment, impaired social or occupational functioning) that developed during, or shortly after, alcohol ingestion.

C. One (or more) of the following signs, developing during, or shortly after, alcohol use:

(1) slurred speech
(2) incoordination
(3) unsteady gait
(4) nystagmus
(5) impairment in attention or memory
(6) stupor or coma

D. The symptoms are not due to a general medical condition and are not better accounted for by another mental disorder.

■ 291.81   Alcohol Withdrawal

A. Cessation of (or reduction in) alcohol use that has been heavy and prolonged.

B. Two (or more) of the following, developing within several hours to a few days after Criterion A:

(1) autonomic hyperactivity (e.g., sweating or pulse rate greater than 100)

(2) increased hand tremor

(3) insomnia

(4) nausea or vomiting

(5) transient visual, tactile, or auditory hallucinations or illusions

(6) psychomotor agitation

(7) anxiety

(8) grand mal seizures

C. The symptoms in Criterion B cause clinically significant distress or impairment in social, occupational, or other important areas of functioning.

D. The symptoms are not due to a general medical condition and are not better accounted for by another mental disorder.

Specify if:

With Perceptual Disturbances: This specifier may be noted when hallucinations with intact reality testing or auditory, visual, or tactile illusions occur in the absence of a delirium. *Intact reality testing* means that the person knows that the hallucinations are induced by the substance and do not represent external reality. When hallucinations occur in the absence of intact reality testing, a diagnosis of Substance-Induced Psychotic Disorder, With Hallucinations, should be considered.

Amphetamine (or Amphetamine-Like)–Related Disorders

Amphetamine Use Disorders

304.40   **Amphetamine Dependence** (see p. 108 for criteria)
305.70   **Amphetamine Abuse** (see p. 112 for criteria)

Amphetamine-Induced Disorders

292.89   **Amphetamine Intoxication** (see below for criteria)
292.0   **Amphetamine Withdrawal** (see below for criteria)
292.81   **Amphetamine Intoxication Delirium** (see p. 82 for criteria)
292.11   **Amphetamine-Induced Psychotic Disorder, With Delusions** (see p. 157 for criteria) *Specify if:* With Onset During Intoxication
292.12   **Amphetamine-Induced Psychotic Disorder, With Hallucinations** (see p. 157 for criteria) *Specify if:* With Onset During Intoxication
292.84   **Amphetamine-Induced Mood Disorder** (see p. 184 for criteria) *Specify if:* With Onset During Intoxication/With Onset During Withdrawal

292.89   **Amphetamine-Induced Anxiety Disorder** (see p. 215 for criteria) *Specify if:* With Onset During Intoxication

292.89   **Amphetamine-Induced Sexual Dysfunction** (see p. 240 for criteria) *Specify if:* With Onset During Intoxication

292.89   **Amphetamine-Induced Sleep Disorder** (see p. 266 for criteria) *Specify if:* With Onset During Intoxication/With Onset During Withdrawal

292.9   **Amphetamine-Related Disorder Not Otherwise Specified**

The Amphetamine-Related Disorder Not Otherwise Specified category is for disorders associated with the use of amphetamine (or a related substance) that are not classifiable as one of the disorders listed above.

■ 292.89 Amphetamine Intoxication

A. Recent use of amphetamine or a related substance (e.g., methylphenidate).

B. Clinically significant maladaptive behavioral or psychological changes (e.g., euphoria or affective blunting; changes in sociability; hypervigilance; interpersonal sensitivity; anxiety, tension, or anger; stereotyped behaviors; impaired judgment; or impaired social or occupational functioning) that developed during, or shortly after, use of amphetamine or a related substance.

C. Two (or more) of the following, developing during, or shortly after, use of amphetamine or a related substance:

    (1)   tachycardia or bradycardia

    (2)   pupillary dilation

    (3)   elevated or lowered blood pressure

    (4)   perspiration or chills

    (5)   nausea or vomiting

    (6)   evidence of weight loss

    (7)   psychomotor agitation or retardation

    (8)   muscular weakness, respiratory depression, chest pain, or cardiac arrhythmias

    (9)   confusion, seizures, dyskinesias, dystonias, or coma

D. The symptoms are not due to a general medical condition and are not better accounted for by another mental disorder.

Specify if:

    With Perceptual Disturbances: This specifier may be noted when hallucinations with intact reality testing or auditory, visual, or tactile illusions occur in the absence of a delirium. *Intact reality testing* means that the person knows that the hallucinations are induced by the substance and do not represent external reality. When hallucinations occur in the absence of intact reality testing, a diagnosis of Substance-Induced Psychotic Disorder, With Hallucinations, should be considered.

■ 292.0   Amphetamine Withdrawal

A. Cessation of (or reduction in) amphetamine (or a related substance) use that has been heavy and prolonged.

B. Dysphoric mood and two (or more) of the following physiological changes, developing within a few hours to several days after Criterion A:

    (1)   fatigue
    (2)   vivid, unpleasant dreams
    (3)   insomnia or hypersomnia
    (4)   increased appetite
    (5)   psychomotor retardation or agitation

C. The symptoms in Criterion B cause clinically significant distress or impairment in social, occupational, or other important areas of functioning.

D. The symptoms are not due to a general medical condition and are not better accounted for by another mental disorder.

Caffeine-Related Disorders

Caffeine-Induced Disorders

305.90   **Caffeine Intoxication** (see below for criteria)

292.89   **Caffeine-Induced Anxiety Disorder** (see p. 215 for criteria) *Specify if:* With Onset During Intoxication

292.89   **Caffeine-Induced Sleep Disorder** (see p. 266 for criteria) *Specify if:* With Onset During Intoxication

292.9   **Caffeine-Related Disorder Not Otherwise Specified**
The Caffeine-Related Disorder Not Otherwise Specified category is for disorders associated with the use of caffeine that are not classifiable as one of the disorders listed above. An example is caffeine withdrawal (see Appendix B in DSM-IV for suggested research criteria).

■ 305.90 Caffeine Intoxication

A. Recent consumption of caffeine, usually in excess of 250 mg (e.g., more than 2–3 cups of brewed coffee).

B. Five (or more) of the following signs, developing during, or shortly after, caffeine use:

   (1) restlessness
   (2) nervousness
   (3) excitement
   (4) insomnia
   (5) flushed face
   (6) diuresis
   (7) gastrointestinal disturbance
   (8) muscle twitching
   (9) rambling flow of thought and speech
   (10) tachycardia or cardiac arrhythmia
   (11) periods of inexhaustibility
   (12) psychomotor agitation

C. The symptoms in Criterion B cause clinically significant distress or impairment in social, occupational, or other important areas of functioning.

D. The symptoms are not due to a general medical condition and are not better accounted for by another mental disorder (e.g., an Anxiety Disorder).

Cannabis-Related Disorders

Cannabis Use Disorders

304.30 **Cannabis Dependence** (see p. 108 for criteria)
305.20 **Cannabis Abuse** (see p. 112 for criteria)

Cannabis-Induced Disorders

292.89 **Cannabis Intoxication** (see below for criteria)

292.81 **Cannabis Intoxication Delirium** (see p. 82 for criteria)

292.11 **Cannabis-Induced Psychotic Disorder, With Delusions** (see p. 157 for criteria) *Specify if:* With Onset During Intoxication

292.12 **Cannabis-Induced Psychotic Disorder, With Hallucinations** (see p. 157 for criteria) *Specify if:* With Onset During Intoxication

292.89 **Cannabis-Induced Anxiety Disorder** (see p. 215 for criteria) *Specify if:* With Onset During Intoxication

292.9 **Cannabis-Related Disorder Not Otherwise Specified**
The Cannabis-Related Disorder Not Otherwise Specified category is for disorders associated with the use of cannabis that are not classifiable as one of the disorders listed above.

■ 292.89 Cannabis Intoxication

A. Recent use of cannabis.

B. Clinically significant maladaptive behavioral or psychological changes (e.g., impaired motor coordination, euphoria, anxiety, sensation of slowed time, impaired judgment, social withdrawal) that developed during, or shortly after, cannabis use.

C. Two (or more) of the following signs, developing within 2 hours of cannabis use:

    (1)   conjunctival injection
    (2)   increased appetite
    (3)   dry mouth
    (4)   tachycardia

D. The symptoms are not due to a general medical condition and are not better accounted for by another mental disorder.

Specify if:

> **With Perceptual Disturbances:** This specifier may be noted when hallucinations with intact reality testing or auditory, visual, or tactile illusions occur in the absence of a delirium. *Intact reality testing* means that the person knows that the hallucinations are induced by the substance and do not represent external reality. When hallucinations occur in the absence of intact reality testing, a diagnosis of Substance-Induced Psychotic Disorder, With Hallucinations, should be considered.

Cocaine-Related Disorders

Cocaine Use Disorders

304.20 **Cocaine Dependence** (see p. 108 for criteria)
305.60 **Cocaine Abuse** (see p. 112 for criteria)

Cocaine-Induced Disorders

292.89 **Cocaine Intoxication** (see below for criteria)
292.0   **Cocaine Withdrawal** (see below for criteria)
292.81 **Cocaine Intoxication Delirium** (see p. 82 for criteria)

**292.11   Cocaine-Induced Psychotic Disorder, With
Delusions** (see p. 157 for criteria) *Specify if:*
With Onset During Intoxication

**292.12   Cocaine-Induced Psychotic Disorder, With
Hallucinations** (see p. 157 for criteria)
Specify if: With Onset During Intoxication

292.84   Cocaine-Induced Mood Disorder (see p. 184
for criteria) *Specify if:* With Onset During
Intoxication/With Onset During Withdrawal

292.89   Cocaine-Induced Anxiety Disorder
(see p. 215 for criteria) *Specify if:* With Onset
During Intoxication/With Onset During
Withdrawal

292.89   Cocaine-Induced Sexual Dysfunction (see
p. 240 for criteria) *Specify if:* With Onset During
Intoxication

292.89   Cocaine-Induced Sleep Disorder (see p. 266 for
criteria) *Specify if:* With Onset During
Intoxication/With Onset During Withdrawal

**292.9   Cocaine-Related Disorder Not Otherwise
Specified**
The Cocaine-Related Disorder Not Otherwise
Specified category is for disorders associated
with the use of cocaine that are not classifiable
as one of the disorders listed above.

■ 292.89   Cocaine Intoxication

A. Recent use of cocaine.

B. Clinically significant maladaptive behavioral or psychological changes (e.g., euphoria or affective blunting;
changes in sociability; hypervigilance; interpersonal

sensitivity; anxiety, tension, or anger; stereotyped behaviors; impaired judgment; or impaired social or occupational functioning) that developed during, or shortly
after, use of cocaine.

C. Two (or more) of the following, developing during, or
shortly after, cocaine use:

(1) tachycardia or bradycardia
(2) pupillary dilation
(3) elevated or lowered blood pressure
(4) perspiration or chills
(5) nausea or vomiting
(6) evidence of weight loss
(7) psychomotor agitation or retardation
(8) muscular weakness, respiratory depression, chest
pain, or cardiac arrhythmias
(9) confusion, seizures, dyskinesias, dystonias, or
coma

D. The symptoms are not due to a general medical condition and are not better accounted for by another mental
disorder.

Specify if:
With Perceptual Disturbances: This specifier may be
noted when hallucinations with intact reality testing
or auditory, visual, or tactile illusions occur in the
absence of a delirium. *Intact reality testing* means that
the person knows that the hallucinations are induced
by the substance and do not represent external reality.
When hallucinations occur in the absence of intact
reality testing, a diagnosis of Substance-Induced
Psychotic Disorder, With Hallucinations, should be
considered.

■ 292.0   Cocaine Withdrawal

A. Cessation of (or reduction in) cocaine use that has been heavy and prolonged.

B. Dysphoric mood and two (or more) of the following physiological changes, developing within a few hours to several days after Criterion A:

(1) fatigue
(2) vivid, unpleasant dreams
(3) insomnia or hypersomnia
(4) increased appetite
(5) psychomotor retardation or agitation

C. The symptoms in Criterion B cause clinically significant distress or impairment in social, occupational, or other important areas of functioning.

D. The symptoms are not due to a general medical condition and are not better accounted for by another mental disorder.

Hallucinogen-Related Disorders

Hallucinogen Use Disorders

304.50   Hallucinogen Dependence (see p. 108 for criteria)
305.30   Hallucinogen Abuse (see p. 112 for criteria)

Hallucinogen-Induced Disorders

292.89   Hallucinogen Intoxication (see below for criteria)

292.89   **Hallucinogen Persisting Perception Disorder (Flashbacks)** (see below for criteria)

292.81   **Hallucinogen Intoxication Delirium** (see p. 82 for criteria)

292.11   **Hallucinogen-Induced Psychotic Disorder, With Delusions** (see p. 157 for criteria) *Specify if:* With Onset During Intoxication

292.12   **Hallucinogen-Induced Psychotic Disorder, With Hallucinations** (see p. 157 for criteria) *Specify if:* With Onset During Intoxication

292.84   **Hallucinogen-Induced Mood Disorder** (see p. 184 for criteria) *Specify if:* With Onset During Intoxication

292.89   **Hallucinogen-Induced Anxiety Disorder** (see p. 215 for criteria) *Specify if:* With Onset During Intoxication

292.9   **Hallucinogen-Related Disorder Not Otherwise Specified**
The Hallucinogen-Related Disorder Not Otherwise Specified category is for disorders associated with the use of hallucinogens that are not classifiable as one of the disorders listed above.

■ 292.89   Hallucinogen Intoxication

A.   Recent use of a hallucinogen.

B.   Clinically significant maladaptive behavioral or psychological changes (e.g., marked anxiety or depression, ideas of reference, fear of losing one's mind, paranoid ideation, impaired judgment, or impaired social or occupational functioning) that developed during, or shortly after, hallucinogen use.

C. Perceptual changes occurring in a state of full wakefulness and alertness (e.g., subjective intensification of perceptions, depersonalization, derealization, illusions, hallucinations, synesthesias) that developed during, or shortly after, hallucinogen use.

D. Two (or more) of the following signs, developing during, or shortly after, hallucinogen use:

    (1) pupillary dilation
    (2) tachycardia
    (3) sweating
    (4) palpitations
    (5) blurring of vision
    (6) tremors
    (7) incoordination

E. The symptoms are not due to a general medical condition and are not better accounted for by another mental disorder.

■ 292.89 Hallucinogen Persisting Perception Disorder (Flashbacks)

A. The reexperiencing, following cessation of use of a hallucinogen, of one or more of the perceptual symptoms that were experienced while intoxicated with the hallucinogen (e.g., geometric hallucinations, false perceptions of movement in the peripheral visual fields, flashes of color, intensified colors, trails of images of moving objects, positive afterimages, halos around objects, macropsia, and micropsia).

B. The symptoms in Criterion A cause clinically significant distress or impairment in social, occupational, or other important areas of functioning.

C. The symptoms are not due to a general medical condition (e.g., anatomical lesions and infections of the brain, visual epilepsies) and are not better accounted for by another mental disorder (e.g., delirium, dementia, Schizophrenia) or hypnopompic hallucinations.

Inhalant-Related Disorders

Inhalant Use Disorders

304.60 Inhalant Dependence (see p. 108 for criteria)
305.90 Inhalant Abuse (see p. 112 for criteria)

Inhalant-Induced Disorders

292.89 Inhalant Intoxication (see below for criteria)
292.81 Inhalant Intoxication Delirium (see p. 82 for criteria)
292.82 Inhalant-Induced Persisting Dementia (see p. 91 for criteria)
292.11 Inhalant-Induced Psychotic Disorder, With Delusions (see p. 157 for criteria) *Specify if:* With Onset During Intoxication
292.12 Inhalant-Induced Psychotic Disorder, With Hallucinations (see p. 157 for criteria) *Specify if:* With Onset During Intoxication
292.84 Inhalant-Induced Mood Disorder (see p. 184 for criteria) *Specify if:* With Onset During Intoxication
292.89 Inhalant-Induced Anxiety Disorder (see p. 215 for criteria) *Specify if:* With Onset During Intoxication

292.9   Inhalant-Related Disorder Not Otherwise Specified

The Inhalant-Related Disorder Not Otherwise Specified category is for disorders associated with the use of inhalants that are not classifiable as one of the disorders listed above.

■ 292.89   Inhalant Intoxication

A. Recent intentional use or short-term, high-dose exposure to volatile inhalants (excluding anesthetic gases and short-acting vasodilators).

B. Clinically significant maladaptive behavioral or psychological changes (e.g., belligerence, assaultiveness, apathy, impaired judgment, impaired social or occupational functioning) that developed during, or shortly after, use of or exposure to volatile inhalants.

C. Two (or more) of the following signs, developing during, or shortly after, inhalant use or exposure:

   (1)   dizziness
   (2)   nystagmus
   (3)   incoordination
   (4)   slurred speech
   (5)   unsteady gait
   (6)   lethargy
   (7)   depressed reflexes
   (8)   psychomotor retardation
   (9)   tremor
   (10) generalized muscle weakness
   (11) blurred vision or diplopia
   (12) stupor or coma
   (13) euphoria

D. The symptoms are not due to a general medical condition and are not better accounted for by another mental disorder.

Nicotine-Related Disorders

Nicotine Use Disorder

305.10   Nicotine Dependence (see p. 108 for criteria)

Nicotine-Induced Disorder

292.0   Nicotine Withdrawal (see below for criteria)

292.9   Nicotine-Related Disorder Not Otherwise Specified
The Nicotine-Related Disorder Not Otherwise Specified category is for disorders associated with the use of nicotine that are not classifiable as Nicotine Dependence or Nicotine Withdrawal.

■ 292.0   Nicotine Withdrawal

A. Daily use of nicotine for at least several weeks.

B. Abrupt cessation of nicotine use, or reduction in the amount of nicotine used, followed within 24 hours by four (or more) of the following signs:
    (1) dysphoric or depressed mood
    (2) insomnia
    (3) irritability, frustration, or anger
    (4) anxiety
    (5) difficulty concentrating

    (6)   restlessness
    (7)   decreased heart rate
    (8)   increased appetite or weight gain

C. The symptoms in Criterion B cause clinically significant distress or impairment in social, occupational, or other important areas of functioning.

D. The symptoms are not due to a general medical condition and are not better accounted for by another mental disorder.

Opioid-Related Disorders

Opioid Use Disorders

304.00 **Opioid Dependence** (see p. 108 for criteria)
305.50 **Opioid Abuse** (see p. 112 for criteria)

Opioid-Induced Disorders

292.89 **Opioid Intoxication** (see below for criteria)
292.0   **Opioid Withdrawal** (see below for criteria)
292.81 **Opioid Intoxication Delirium** (see p. 82 for criteria)
292.11 **Opioid-Induced Psychotic Disorder, With Delusions** (see p. 157 for criteria) *Specify if:* With Onset During Intoxication
292.12 **Opioid-Induced Psychotic Disorder, With Hallucinations** (see p. 157 for criteria) *Specify if:* With Onset During Intoxication
292.84 **Opioid-Induced Mood Disorder** (see p. 184 for criteria) *Specify if:* With Onset During Intoxication

292.89 **Opioid-Induced Sexual Dysfunction** (see
p. 240 for criteria) *Specify if:* With Onset During
Intoxication

292.89 **Opioid-Induced Sleep Disorder** (see p. 266
for criteria) *Specify if:* With Onset During
Intoxication/With Onset During Withdrawal

292.9 **Opioid-Related Disorder Not Otherwise
Specified**

The Opioid-Related Disorder Not Otherwise
Specified category is for disorders associated
with the use of opioids that are not classifiable
as one of the disorders listed above.

■ 292.89 Opioid Intoxication

A. Recent use of an opioid.

B. Clinically significant maladaptive behavioral or psychological changes (e.g., initial euphoria followed by apathy, dysphoria, psychomotor agitation or retardation,
impaired judgment, or impaired social or occupational
functioning) that developed during, or shortly after,
opioid use.

C. Pupillary constriction (or pupillary dilation due to an-
oxia from severe overdose) and one (or more) of the
following signs, developing during, or shortly after,
opioid use:

   (1) drowsiness or coma
   (2) slurred speech
   (3) impairment in attention or memory

D. The symptoms are not due to a general medical condition and are not better accounted for by another mental disorder.

Specify if:

With Perceptual Disturbances: This specifier may be noted when hallucinations with intact reality testing or auditory, visual, or tactile illusions occur in the absence of a delirium. *Intact reality testing* means that the person knows that the hallucinations are induced by the substance and do not represent external reality. When hallucinations occur in the absence of intact reality testing, a diagnosis of Substance-Induced Psychotic Disorder, With Hallucinations, should be considered.

■ 292.0 Opioid Withdrawal

A. Either of the following:
   (1) cessation of (or reduction in) opioid use that has been heavy and prolonged (several weeks or longer)
   (2) administration of an opioid antagonist after a period of opioid use

B. Three (or more) of the following, developing within minutes to several days after Criterion A:
   (1) dysphoric mood
   (2) nausea or vomiting
   (3) muscle aches
   (4) lacrimation or rhinorrhea
   (5) pupillary dilation, piloerection, or sweating
   (6) diarrhea
   (7) yawning

(8) fever
(9) insomnia

C. The symptoms in Criterion B cause clinically significant distress or impairment in social, occupational, or other important areas of functioning.

D. The symptoms are not due to a general medical condition and are not better accounted for by another mental disorder.

Phencyclidine (or Phencyclidine-Like)–Related Disorders

Phencyclidine Use Disorders

304.60 Phencyclidine Dependence (see p. 108 for criteria)
305.90 Phencyclidine Abuse (see p. 112 for criteria)

Phencyclidine-Induced Disorders

292.89 Phencyclidine Intoxication (see below for criteria)
292.81 Phencyclidine Intoxication Delirium (see p. 82 for criteria)
292.11 Phencyclidine-Induced Psychotic Disorder, With Delusions (see p. 157 for criteria) *Specify if:* With Onset During Intoxication
292.12 Phencyclidine-Induced Psychotic Disorder, With Hallucinations (see p. 157 for criteria) *Specify if:* With Onset During Intoxication

292.84   Phencyclidine-Induced Mood Disorder (see p. 184 for criteria) *Specify if:* With Onset During Intoxication

292.89   Phencyclidine-Induced Anxiety Disorder (see p. 215 for criteria) *Specify if:* With Onset During Intoxication

292.9   Phencyclidine-Related Disorder Not Otherwise Specified

The Phencyclidine-Related Disorder Not Otherwise Specified category is for disorders associated with the use of phencyclidine that are not classifiable as one of the disorders listed above.

■ 292.89   Phencyclidine Intoxication

A. Recent use of phencyclidine (or a related substance).

B. Clinically significant maladaptive behavioral changes (e.g., belligerence, assaultiveness, impulsiveness, unpredictability, psychomotor agitation, impaired judgment, or impaired social or occupational functioning) that developed during, or shortly after, phencyclidine use.

C. Within an hour (less when smoked, "snorted," or used intravenously), two (or more) of the following signs:

(1) vertical or horizontal nystagmus
(2) hypertension or tachycardia
(3) numbness or diminished responsiveness to pain
(4) ataxia
(5) dysarthria
(6) muscle rigidity
(7) seizures or coma
(8) hyperacusis

D. The symptoms are not due to a general medical condition and are not better accounted for by another mental disorder.

Specify if:

 With Perceptual Disturbances: This specifier may be noted when hallucinations with intact reality testing or auditory, visual, or tactile illusions occur in the absence of a delirium. *Intact reality testing* means that the person knows that the hallucinations are induced by the substance and do not represent external reality. When hallucinations occur in the absence of intact reality testing, a diagnosis of Substance-Induced Psychotic Disorder, With Hallucinations, should be considered.

Sedative-, Hypnotic-, or Anxiolytic-Related Disorders

Sedative, Hypnotic, or Anxiolytic Use Disorders

304.10 **Sedative, Hypnotic, or Anxiolytic Dependence** (see p. 108 for criteria)

305.40 **Sedative, Hypnotic, or Anxiolytic Abuse** (see p. 112 for criteria)

Sedative-, Hypnotic-, or Anxiolytic-Induced Disorders

292.89 **Sedative, Hypnotic, or Anxiolytic Intoxication** (see below for criteria)

292.0 **Sedative, Hypnotic, or Anxiolytic Withdrawal** (see below for criteria)

292.81   **Sedative, Hypnotic, or Anxiolytic Intoxication Delirium** (see p. 82 for criteria)

292.81   **Sedative, Hypnotic, or Anxiolytic Withdrawal Delirium** (see p. 83 for criteria)

292.82   **Sedative-, Hypnotic-, or Anxiolytic-Induced Persisting Dementia** (see p. 91 for criteria)

292.83   **Sedative-, Hypnotic-, or Anxiolytic-Induced Persisting Amnestic Disorder** (see p. 94 for criteria)

292.11   **Sedative-, Hypnotic-, or Anxiolytic-Induced Psychotic Disorder, With Delusions** (see p. 157 for criteria) *Specify if:* With Onset During Intoxication/With Onset During Withdrawal

292.12   **Sedative-, Hypnotic-, or Anxiolytic-Induced Psychotic Disorder, With Hallucinations** (see p. 157 for criteria) *Specify if:* With Onset During Intoxication/With Onset During Withdrawal

292.84   **Sedative-, Hypnotic-, or Anxiolytic-Induced Mood Disorder** (see p. 184 for criteria) *Specify if:* With Onset During Intoxication/With Onset During Withdrawal

292.89   **Sedative-, Hypnotic-, or Anxiolytic-Induced Anxiety Disorder** (see p. 215 for criteria) *Specify if:* With Onset During Withdrawal

292.89   **Sedative-, Hypnotic-, or Anxiolytic-Induced Sexual Dysfunction** (see p. 240 for criteria) *Specify if:* With Onset During Intoxication

292.89   **Sedative-, Hypnotic-, or Anxiolytic-Induced Sleep Disorder** (see p. 266 for criteria) *Specify if:* With Onset During Intoxication/With Onset During Withdrawal

292.9   **Sedative-, Hypnotic-, or Anxiolytic-Related Disorder Not Otherwise Specified**

The Sedative-, Hypnotic-, or Anxiolytic-Related Disorder Not Otherwise Specified category is for disorders associated with the use of sedatives, hypnotics, or anxiolytics that are not classifiable as one of the disorders listed above.

■ 292.89   Sedative, Hypnotic, or Anxiolytic Intoxication

A.   Recent use of a sedative, hypnotic, or anxiolytic.

B.   Clinically significant maladaptive behavioral or psychological changes (e.g., inappropriate sexual or aggressive behavior, mood lability, impaired judgment, impaired social or occupational functioning) that developed during, or shortly after, sedative, hypnotic, or anxiolytic use.

C.   One (or more) of the following signs, developing during, or shortly after, sedative, hypnotic, or anxiolytic use:

     (1)   slurred speech
     (2)   incoordination
     (3)   unsteady gait
     (4)   nystagmus
     (5)   impairment in attention or memory
     (6)   stupor or coma

D.   The symptoms are not due to a general medical condition and are not better accounted for by another mental disorder.

■ 292.0 Sedative, Hypnotic, or Anxiolytic Withdrawal

A. Cessation of (or reduction in) sedative, hypnotic, or anxiolytic use that has been heavy and prolonged.

B. Two (or more) of the following, developing within several hours to a few days after Criterion A:

(1) autonomic hyperactivity (e.g., sweating or pulse rate greater than 100)
(2) increased hand tremor
(3) insomnia
(4) nausea or vomiting
(5) transient visual, tactile, or auditory hallucinations or illusions
(6) psychomotor agitation
(7) anxiety
(8) grand mal seizures

C. The symptoms in Criterion B cause clinically significant distress or impairment in social, occupational, or other important areas of functioning.

D. The symptoms are not due to a general medical condition and are not better accounted for by another mental disorder.

Specify if:

With Perceptual Disturbances: This specifier may be noted when hallucinations with intact reality testing or auditory, visual, or tactile illusions occur in the absence of a delirium. *Intact reality testing* means that the person knows that the hallucinations are induced by the substance and do not represent external reality. When hallucinations occur in the absence of intact reality testing, a diagnosis of Substance-Induced Psychotic Disorder, With Hallucinations, should be considered.

Polysubstance-Related Disorder

■ 304.80 Polysubstance Dependence

This diagnosis is reserved for behavior during the same 12-month period in which the person was repeatedly using at least three groups of substances (not including caffeine and nicotine), but no single substance predominated. Further, during this period, the Dependence criteria were met for substances as a group but not for any specific substance.

Other (or Unknown) Substance–Related Disorders

The Other (or Unknown) Substance–Related Disorders category is for classifying Substance-Related Disorders associated with substances not listed in this section. Examples of these substances include anabolic steroids, nitrite inhalants ("poppers"), nitrous oxide, over-the-counter and prescription medications not otherwise covered by the 11 categories (e.g., cortisol, antihistamines, benztropine), and other substances that have psychoactive effects. In addition, this category may be used when the specific substance is unknown (e.g., an intoxication after taking a bottle of unlabeled pills). A discussion of how to code medication-related disorders is found on p. 114.

Other (or Unknown) Substance Use Disorders

304.90   **Other (or Unknown) Substance Dependence**
(see p. 108 for criteria)

305.90   **Other (or Unknown) Substance Abuse** (see
p. 112 for criteria)

Other (or Unknown) Substance–Induced Disorders

292.89   **Other (or Unknown) Substance Intoxication**
(see p. 113 for criteria) *Specify if:* With
Perceptual Disturbances

292.0   **Other (or Unknown) Substance Withdrawal**
(see p. 113 for criteria) *Specify if:* With
Perceptual Disturbances

292.81   **Other (or Unknown) Substance-Induced
Delirium** (see p. 82 for criteria)

292.82   **Other (or Unknown) Substance–Induced
Persisting Dementia** (see p. 91 for criteria)

292.83   **Other (or Unknown) Substance–Induced
Persisting Amnestic Disorder** (see p. 94 for
criteria)

292.11   **Other (or Unknown) Substance–Induced
Psychotic Disorder, With Delusions** (see
p. 157 for criteria) *Specify if:* With Onset
During Intoxication/With Onset During
Withdrawal

292.12   **Other (or Unknown) Substance–Induced
Psychotic Disorder, With Hallucinations**
(see p. 157 for criteria) *Specify if:* With Onset
During Intoxication/With Onset During
Withdrawal

292.84   **Other (or Unknown) Substance–Induced Mood Disorder** (see p. 184 for criteria) *Specify if:* With Onset During Intoxication/With Onset During Withdrawal

292.89   **Other (or Unknown) Substance–Induced Anxiety Disorder** (see p. 215 for criteria) *Specify if:* With Onset During Intoxication/With Onset During Withdrawal

292.89   **Other (or Unknown) Substance–Induced Sexual Dysfunction** (see p. 240 for criteria) *Specify if:* With Onset During Intoxication

292.89   **Other (or Unknown) Substance–Induced Sleep Disorder** (see p. 266 for criteria) *Specify if:* With Onset During Intoxication/With Onset During Withdrawal

292.9   **Other (or Unknown) Substance–Related Disorder Not Otherwise Specified**

Schizophrenia and Other Psychotic Disorders

■ Schizophrenia

A. *Characteristic symptoms:* Two (or more) of the following, each present for a significant portion of time during a 1-month period (or less if successfully treated):

    (1)   delusions
    (2)   hallucinations
    (3)   disorganized speech (e.g., frequent derailment or incoherence)
    (4)   grossly disorganized or catatonic behavior
    (5)   negative symptoms, i.e., affective flattening, alogia, or avolition

Note: Only one Criterion A symptom is required if delusions are bizarre or hallucinations consist of a voice keeping up a running commentary on the person's behavior or thoughts, or two or more voices conversing with each other.

B. *Social/occupational dysfunction:* For a significant portion of the time since the onset of the disturbance, one or more major areas of functioning such as work, interpersonal relations, or self-care are markedly below the level achieved prior to the onset (or when the onset is in childhood or adolescence, failure to achieve expected level of interpersonal, academic, or occupational achievement).

C. *Duration:* Continuous signs of the disturbance persist for at least 6 months. This 6-month period must include at least 1 month of symptoms (or less if successfully treated) that meet Criterion A (i.e., active-phase symptoms) and may include periods of prodromal or residual symptoms. During these prodromal or residual periods, the signs of the disturbance may be manifested by only negative symptoms or two or more symptoms listed in Criterion A present in an attenuated form (e.g., odd beliefs, unusual perceptual experiences).

D. *Schizoaffective and Mood Disorder exclusion:* Schizoaffective Disorder and Mood Disorder With Psychotic Features have been ruled out because either (1) no Major Depressive, Manic, or Mixed Episodes have occurred concurrently with the active-phase symptoms; or (2) if mood episodes have occurred during active-phase symptoms, their total duration has been brief relative to the duration of the active and residual periods.

E. *Substance/general medical condition exclusion:* The disturbance is not due to the direct physiological effects of a substance (e.g., a drug of abuse, a medication) or a general medical condition.

F. *Relationship to a Pervasive Developmental Disorder:* If there is a history of Autistic Disorder or another Pervasive Developmental Disorder, the additional diagnosis of Schizophrenia is made only if prominent delusions or hallucinations are also present for at least a month (or less if successfully treated).

Schizophrenia Subtypes

The subtypes of Schizophrenia are defined by the predominant symptomatology at the time of evaluation.

☐ 295.30 Paranoid Type

A type of Schizophrenia in which the following criteria are met:

A. Preoccupation with one or more delusions or frequent auditory hallucinations.

B. None of the following is prominent: disorganized speech, disorganized or catatonic behavior, or flat or inappropriate affect.

☐ 295.10 Disorganized Type

A type of Schizophrenia in which the following criteria are met:

A. All of the following are prominent:
  (1) disorganized speech
  (2) disorganized behavior
  (3) flat or inappropriate affect

B. The criteria are not met for Catatonic Type.

☐ 295.20 Catatonic Type

A type of Schizophrenia in which the clinical picture is dominated by at least two of the following:

   (1)   motoric immobility as evidenced by catalepsy (in-
         cluding waxy flexibility) or stupor
   (2)   excessive motor activity (that is apparently pur-
         poseless and not influenced by external stimuli)
   (3)   extreme negativism (an apparently motiveless re-
         sistance to all instructions or maintenance of a rigid
         posture against attempts to be moved) or mutism
   (4)   peculiarities of voluntary movement as evidenced
         by posturing (voluntary assumption of inappropri-
         ate or bizarre postures), stereotyped movements,
         prominent mannerisms, or prominent grimacing
   (5)   echolalia or echopraxia

☐ 295.90 Undifferentiated Type

A type of Schizophrenia in which symptoms that meet
Criterion A are present, but the criteria are not met for the
Paranoid, Disorganized, or Catatonic Type.

☐ 295.60 Residual Type

A type of Schizophrenia in which the following criteria
are met:

A. Absence of prominent delusions, hallucinations, disor-
    ganized speech, and grossly disorganized or catatonic
    behavior.

B. There is continuing evidence of the disturbance, as
    indicated by the presence of negative symptoms or two
    or more symptoms listed in Criterion A for Schizophre-
    nia, present in an attenuated form (e.g., odd beliefs,
    unusual perceptual experiences).

Classification of Longitudinal Course for Schizophrenia

These specifiers can be applied only after at least 1 year has elapsed since the initial onset of active-phase symptoms:

Episodic With Interepisode Residual Symptoms: when the course is characterized by episodes in which Criterion A for Schizophrenia is met and there are clinically significant residual symptoms between the episodes. **With Prominent Negative Symptoms** can be added if prominent negative symptoms are present during these residual periods.

Episodic With No Interepisode Residual Symptoms: when the course is characterized by episodes in which Criterion A for Schizophrenia is met and there are no clinically significant residual symptoms between the episodes.

Continuous: when characteristic symptoms of Criterion A are met throughout all (or most) of the course. **With Prominent Negative Symptoms** can be added if prominent negative symptoms are also present.

Single Episode In Partial Remission: when there has been a single episode in which Criterion A for Schizophrenia is met and some clinically significant residual symptoms remain. **With Prominent Negative Symptoms** can be added if these residual symptoms include prominent negative symptoms.

Single Episode In Full Remission: when there has been a single episode in which Criterion A for Schizophrenia has been met and no clinically significant residual symptoms remain.

Other or Unspecified Pattern: if another or an unspecified course pattern has been present.

■ 295.40   Schizophreniform Disorder

A.   Criteria A, D, and E of Schizophrenia are met.

B.   An episode of the disorder (including prodromal, active, and residual phases) lasts at least 1 month but less than 6 months. (When the diagnosis must be made without waiting for recovery, it should be qualified as "Provisional.")

Specify if:
   Without Good Prognostic Features
   With Good Prognostic Features: as evidenced by two (or more) of the following:

   (1)   onset of prominent psychotic symptoms within 4 weeks of the first noticeable change in usual behavior or functioning
   (2)   confusion or perplexity at the height of the psychotic episode
   (3)   good premorbid social and occupational functioning
   (4)   absence of blunted or flat affect

■ 295.70   Schizoaffective Disorder

A.   An uninterrupted period of illness during which, at some time, there is either a Major Depressive Episode, a Manic Episode, or a Mixed Episode concurrent with symptoms that meet Criterion A for Schizophrenia.

   Note: The Major Depressive Episode must include Criterion A1: depressed mood.

B.   During the same period of illness, there have been delusions or hallucinations for at least 2 weeks in the absence of prominent mood symptoms.

C. Symptoms that meet criteria for a mood episode are present for a substantial portion of the total duration of the active and residual periods of the illness.

D. The disturbance is not due to the direct physiological effects of a substance (e.g., a drug of abuse, a medication) or a general medical condition.

Specify type:

Bipolar Type: if the disturbance includes a Manic or a Mixed Episode (or a Manic or a Mixed Episode and Major Depressive Episodes)

Depressive Type: if the disturbance only includes Major Depressive Episodes

■ 297.1 Delusional Disorder

A. Nonbizarre delusions (i.e., involving situations that occur in real life, such as being followed, poisoned, infected, loved at a distance, or deceived by spouse or lover, or having a disease) of at least 1 month's duration.

B. Criterion A for Schizophrenia has never been met. **Note:** Tactile and olfactory hallucinations may be present in Delusional Disorder if they are related to the delusional theme.

C. Apart from the impact of the delusion(s) or its ramifications, functioning is not markedly impaired and behavior is not obviously odd or bizarre.

D. If mood episodes have occurred concurrently with delusions, their total duration has been brief relative to the duration of the delusional periods.

E. The disturbance is not due to the direct physiological effects of a substance (e.g., a drug of abuse, a medication) or a general medical condition.

Specify type (the following types are assigned based on the predominant delusional theme):

Erotomanic Type: delusions that another person, usually of higher status, is in love with the individual

Grandiose Type: delusions of inflated worth, power, knowledge, identity, or special relationship to a deity or famous person

Jealous Type: delusions that the individual's sexual partner is unfaithful

Persecutory Type: delusions that the person (or someone to whom the person is close) is being malevolently treated in some way

Somatic Type: delusions that the person has some physical defect or general medical condition

Mixed Type: delusions characteristic of more than one of the above types but no one theme predominates

Unspecified Type

■ 298.8 Brief Psychotic Disorder

A. Presence of one (or more) of the following symptoms:

(1) delusions

(2) hallucinations

(3) disorganized speech (e.g., frequent derailment or incoherence)

(4) grossly disorganized or catatonic behavior

Note: Do not include a symptom if it is a culturally sanctioned response pattern.

B. Duration of an episode of the disturbance is at least 1 day but less than 1 month, with eventual full return to premorbid level of functioning.

C. The disturbance is not better accounted for by a Mood Disorder With Psychotic Features, Schizoaffective Disorder, or Schizophrenia and is not due to the direct physiological effects of a substance (e.g., a drug of abuse, a medication) or a general medical condition.

Specify if:

With Marked Stressor(s) (brief reactive psychosis): if symptoms occur shortly after and apparently in response to events that, singly or together, would be markedly stressful to almost anyone in similar circumstances in the person's culture

Without Marked Stressor(s): if psychotic symptoms do *not* occur shortly after, or are not apparently in response to events that, singly or together, would be markedly stressful to almost anyone in similar circumstances in the person's culture

With Postpartum Onset: if onset within 4 weeks postpartum

■ 297.3 Shared Psychotic Disorder (Folie à Deux)

A. A delusion develops in an individual in the context of a close relationship with another person(s), who has an already-established delusion.

B. The delusion is similar in content to that of the person who already has the established delusion.

C. The disturbance is not better accounted for by another Psychotic Disorder (e.g., Schizophrenia) or a Mood Disorder With Psychotic Features and is not due to the direct physiological effects of a substance (e.g., a drug of abuse, a medication) or a general medical condition.

■ 293.xx   Psychotic Disorder Due to . . . [*Indicate the General Medical Condition*]

A. Prominent hallucinations or delusions.

B. There is evidence from the history, physical examination, or laboratory findings that the disturbance is the direct physiological consequence of a general medical condition.

C. The disturbance is not better accounted for by another mental disorder.

D. The disturbance does not occur exclusively during the course of a delirium.

Code based on predominant symptom:

.81 With Delusions: if delusions are the predominant symptom

.82 With Hallucinations: if hallucinations are the predominant symptom

Coding note: Include the name of the general medical condition on Axis I, e.g., 293.81 Psychotic Disorder Due to Malignant Lung Neoplasm, With Delusions; also code the general medical condition on Axis III (see Appendix G for codes).

Coding note: If delusions are part of a preexisting dementia, indicate the delusions by coding the appropriate subtype of the dementia if one is available, e.g., 290.20 Dementia of the Alzheimer's Type, With Late Onset, With Delusions.

■ Substance-Induced Psychotic Disorder

A. Prominent hallucinations or delusions. **Note:** Do not include hallucinations if the person has insight that they are substance induced.

B. There is evidence from the history, physical examination, or laboratory findings of either (1) or (2):

   (1) the symptoms in Criterion A developed during, or within a month of, Substance Intoxication or Withdrawal

   (2) medication use is etiologically related to the disturbance

C. The disturbance is not better accounted for by a Psychotic Disorder that is not substance induced. Evidence that the symptoms are better accounted for by a Psychotic Disorder that is not substance induced might include the following: the symptoms precede the onset of the substance use (or medication use); the symptoms persist for a substantial period of time (e.g., about a month) after the cessation of acute withdrawal or severe intoxication, or are substantially in excess of what would be expected given the type or amount of the substance used or the duration of use; or there is other evidence that suggests the existence of an independent non-substance-induced Psychotic Disorder (e.g., a history of recurrent non-substance-related episodes).

D. The disturbance does not occur exclusively during the course of a delirium.

Note: This diagnosis should be made instead of a diagnosis of Substance Intoxication or Substance Withdrawal only when the symptoms are in excess of those usually associated with the intoxication or withdrawal syndrome and when the symptoms are sufficiently severe to warrant independent clinical attention.

Code [Specific Substance]–Induced Psychotic Disorder:
(291.5 Alcohol, With Delusions; 291.3 Alcohol, With Hallucinations; 292.11 Amphetamine [or Amphetamine-Like Substance], With Delusions; 292.12 Amphetamine [or Amphetamine-Like Substance], With Hallucinations; 292.11 Cannabis, With Delusions; 292.12 Cannabis, With Hallucinations; 292.11 Cocaine, With Delusions; 292.12 Cocaine, With Hallucinations; 292.11 Hallucinogen, With Delusions; 292.12 Hallucinogen, With Hallucinations; 292.11 Inhalant, With Delusions; 292.12 Inhalant, With Hallucinations; 292.11 Opioid, With Delusions; 292.12 Opioid, With Hallucinations; 292.11 Phencyclidine [or Phencyclidine-Like Substance], With Delusions; 292.12 Phencyclidine [or Phencyclidine-Like Substance], With Hallucinations; 292.11 Sedative, Hypnotic, or Anxiolytic, With Delusions; 292.12 Sedative, Hypnotic, or Anxiolytic, With Hallucinations; 292.11 Other [or Unknown] Substance, With Delusions; 292.12 Other [or Unknown] Substance, With Hallucinations)

Coding note: The diagnostic code depends on whether the presentation is predominated by delusions or hallucinations. See p. 115 for recording procedures.

Specify if (see table on p. 106 for applicability by substance):
With Onset During Intoxication: if criteria are met for Intoxication with the substance and the symptoms develop during the intoxication syndrome
With Onset During Withdrawal: if criteria are met for Withdrawal from the substance and the symptoms develop during, or shortly after, a withdrawal syndrome

■ 298.9   Psychotic Disorder Not Otherwise Specified

This category includes psychotic symptomatology (i.e., delusions, hallucinations, disorganized speech, grossly disorganized or catatonic behavior) about which there is inadequate information to make a specific diagnosis or about which there is contradictory information, or disorders with psychotic symptoms that do not meet the criteria for any specific Psychotic Disorder.

Examples include

1. Postpartum psychosis that does not meet criteria for Mood Disorder With Psychotic Features, Brief Psychotic Disorder, Psychotic Disorder Due to a General Medical Condition, or Substance-Induced Psychotic Disorder
2. Psychotic symptoms that have lasted for less than 1 month but that have not yet remitted, so that the criteria for Brief Psychotic Disorder are not met
3. Persistent auditory hallucinations in the absence of any other features
4. Persistent nonbizarre delusions with periods of overlapping mood episodes that have been present for a substantial portion of the delusional disturbance
5. Situations in which the clinician has concluded that a Psychotic Disorder is present, but is unable to determine whether it is primary, due to a general medical condition, or substance induced

Mood Disorders

This section is divided into three parts. The first part describes **mood episodes** (Major Depressive Episode, Manic Episode, Mixed Episode, and Hypomanic Episode) that have been included separately at the beginning of this section for convenience in diagnosing the various Mood Disorders. These episodes do not have their own diagnostic codes and cannot be diagnosed as separate entities; however, they serve as the building blocks for the disorder diagnoses. The second part contains criteria sets for the **Mood Disorders** (i.e., Depressive Disorders, Bipolar Disorders, Mood Disorder Due to a General Medical Condition, Substance-Induced Mood Disorder). The criteria sets for most of the Mood Disorders require the presence or absence of the mood episodes described in the first part of the section. The third part includes the **specifiers** that describe either the most recent mood episode or the course of recurrent episodes.

Mood Episodes

☐ Major Depressive Episode

A. Five (or more) of the following symptoms have been present during the same 2-week period and represent a change from previous functioning; at least one of the symptoms is either (1) depressed mood or (2) loss of interest or pleasure.

Note: Do not include symptoms that are clearly due to a general medical condition, or mood-incongruent delusions or hallucinations.

(1)   depressed mood most of the day, nearly every day, as indicated by either subjective report (e.g., feels sad or empty) or observation made by others (e.g., appears tearful). **Note:** In children and adolescents, can be irritable mood.

(2)   markedly diminished interest or pleasure in all, or almost all, activities most of the day, nearly every day (as indicated by either subjective account or observation made by others)

(3)   significant weight loss when not dieting or weight gain (e.g., a change of more than 5% of body weight in a month), or decrease or increase in appetite nearly every day. **Note:** In children, consider failure to make expected weight gains.

(4)   insomnia or hypersomnia nearly every day

(5)   psychomotor agitation or retardation nearly every day (observable by others, not merely subjective feelings of restlessness or being slowed down)

(6)   fatigue or loss of energy nearly every day

(7)   feelings of worthlessness or excessive or inappropriate guilt (which may be delusional) nearly every day (not merely self-reproach or guilt about being sick)

(8)   diminished ability to think or concentrate, or indecisiveness, nearly every day (either by subjective account or as observed by others)

(9)   recurrent thoughts of death (not just fear of dying), recurrent suicidal ideation without a specific plan, or a suicide attempt or a specific plan for committing suicide

B.   The symptoms do not meet criteria for a Mixed Episode (see p. 165).

C.   The symptoms cause clinically significant distress or impairment in social, occupational, or other important areas of functioning.

D.   The symptoms are not due to the direct physiological effects of a substance (e.g., a drug of abuse, a medication) or a general medical condition (e.g., hypothyroidism).

E.   The symptoms are not better accounted for by Bereavement, i.e., after the loss of a loved one, the symptoms persist for longer than 2 months or are characterized by marked functional impairment, morbid preoccupation with worthlessness, suicidal ideation, psychotic symptoms, or psychomotor retardation.

☐ Manic Episode

A.   A distinct period of abnormally and persistently elevated, expansive, or irritable mood, lasting at least 1 week (or any duration if hospitalization is necessary).

B.   During the period of mood disturbance, three (or more) of the following symptoms have persisted (four if the mood is only irritable) and have been present to a significant degree:

(1)   inflated self-esteem or grandiosity

    (2)   decreased need for sleep (e.g., feels rested after only 3 hours of sleep)

    (3)   more talkative than usual or pressure to keep talking

    (4)   flight of ideas or subjective experience that thoughts are racing

    (5)   distractibility (i.e., attention too easily drawn to unimportant or irrelevant external stimuli)

    (6)   increase in goal-directed activity (either socially, at work or school, or sexually) or psychomotor agitation

    (7)   excessive involvement in pleasurable activities that have a high potential for painful consequences (e.g., engaging in unrestrained buying sprees, sexual indiscretions, or foolish business investments)

C.   The symptoms do not meet criteria for a Mixed Episode (see p. 165).

D.   The mood disturbance is sufficiently severe to cause marked impairment in occupational functioning or in usual social activities or relationships with others, or to necessitate hospitalization to prevent harm to self or others, or there are psychotic features.

E.   The symptoms are not due to the direct physiological effects of a substance (e.g., a drug of abuse, a medication, or other treatment) or a general medical condition (e.g., hyperthyroidism).

Note: Manic-like episodes that are clearly caused by somatic antidepressant treatment (e.g., medication, electroconvulsive therapy, light therapy) should not count toward a diagnosis of Bipolar I Disorder.

☐ Mixed Episode

A. The criteria are met both for a Manic Episode (see p. 163) and for a Major Depressive Episode (see p. 161) (except for duration) nearly every day during at least a 1-week period.

B. The mood disturbance is sufficiently severe to cause marked impairment in occupational functioning or in usual social activities or relationships with others, or to necessitate hospitalization to prevent harm to self or others, or there are psychotic features.

C. The symptoms are not due to the direct physiological effects of a substance (e.g., a drug of abuse, a medication, or other treatment) or a general medical condition (e.g., hyperthyroidism).

Note: Mixed-like episodes that are clearly caused by somatic antidepressant treatment (e.g., medication, electroconvulsive therapy, light therapy) should not count toward a diagnosis of Bipolar I Disorder.

☐ Hypomanic Episode

A. A distinct period of persistently elevated, expansive, or irritable mood, lasting throughout at least 4 days, that is clearly different from the usual nondepressed mood.

B. During the period of mood disturbance, three (or more) of the following symptoms have persisted (four if the mood is only irritable) and have been present to a significant degree:

   (1)   inflated self-esteem or grandiosity

   (2)   decreased need for sleep (e.g., feels rested after only 3 hours of sleep)

    (3) more talkative than usual or pressure to keep talking

    (4) flight of ideas or subjective experience that thoughts are racing

    (5) distractibility (i.e., attention too easily drawn to unimportant or irrelevant external stimuli)

    (6) increase in goal-directed activity (either socially, at work or school, or sexually) or psychomotor agitation

    (7) excessive involvement in pleasurable activities that have a high potential for painful consequences (e.g., the person engages in unrestrained buying sprees, sexual indiscretions, or foolish business investments)

C. The episode is associated with an unequivocal change in functioning that is uncharacteristic of the person when not symptomatic.

D. The disturbance in mood and the change in functioning are observable by others.

E. The episode is not severe enough to cause marked impairment in social or occupational functioning, or to necessitate hospitalization, and there are no psychotic features.

F. The symptoms are not due to the direct physiological effects of a substance (e.g., a drug of abuse, a medication, or other treatment) or a general medical condition (e.g., hyperthyroidism).

Note: Hypomanic-like episodes that are clearly caused by somatic antidepressant treatment (e.g., medication, electroconvulsive therapy, light therapy) should not count toward a diagnosis of Bipolar II Disorder.

Depressive Disorders

■ 296.2x   Major Depressive Disorder, Single Episode

A. Presence of a single Major Depressive Episode (see p. 161).

B. The Major Depressive Episode is not better accounted for by Schizoaffective Disorder and is not superimposed on Schizophrenia, Schizophreniform Disorder, Delusional Disorder, or Psychotic Disorder Not Otherwise Specified.

C. There has never been a Manic Episode (see p. 163), a Mixed Episode (see p. 165), or a Hypomanic Episode (see p. 165). **Note:** This exclusion does not apply if all of the manic-like, mixed-like, or hypomanic-like episodes are substance or treatment induced or are due to the direct physiological effects of a general medical condition.

Specify (for current or most recent episode):
   Severity/Psychotic/Remission Specifiers   (see p. 187)
   Chronic (see p. 192)
   With Catatonic Features (see p. 192)
   With Melancholic Features (see p. 193)
   With Atypical Features (see p. 193)
   With Postpartum Onset (see p. 194)

   Coding note: See p. 169 for recording procedures.

■ 296.3x Major Depressive Disorder, Recurrent

A. Presence of two or more Major Depressive Episodes (see p. 161).

   Note: To be considered separate episodes, there must be an interval of at least 2 consecutive months in which criteria are not met for a Major Depressive Episode.

B. The Major Depressive Episodes are not better accounted for by Schizoaffective Disorder and are not superimposed on Schizophrenia, Schizophreniform Disorder, Delusional Disorder, or Psychotic Disorder Not Otherwise Specified.

C. There has never been a Manic Episode (see p. 163), a Mixed Episode (see p. 165), or a Hypomanic Episode (see p. 165). **Note:** This exclusion does not apply if all of the manic-like, mixed-like, or hypomanic-like episodes are substance or treatment induced or are due to the direct physiological effects of a general medical condition.

Specify (for current or most recent episode):
   Severity/Psychotic/Remission Specifiers (see p. 187)
   Chronic (see p. 192)
   With Catatonic Features (see p. 192)
   With Melancholic Features (see p. 193)
   With Atypical Features (see p. 193)
   With Postpartum Onset (see p. 194)

Specify:
   Longitudinal Course Specifiers (With and Without Interepisode Recovery) (see p. 195)
   With Seasonal Pattern (see p. 196)

Recording Procedures

The diagnostic codes for Major Depressive Disorder (Single Episode and Recurrent) are selected as follows:

1. The first three digits are 296.
2. The fourth digit is either 2 (if there is only a single Major Depressive Episode) or 3 (if there are recurrent Major Depressive Episodes).
3. The fifth digit indicates the following: 1 for Mild severity, 2 for Moderate severity, 3 for Severe Without Psychotic Features, 4 for Severe With Psychotic Features, 5 for In Partial Remission, 6 for In Full Remission, and 0 if Unspecified. Other specifiers for Major Depressive Disorder cannot be coded.

In recording the name of a diagnosis, terms should be listed in the following order: Major Depressive Disorder, specifiers coded in the fourth digit (e.g., Recurrent), specifiers coded in the fifth digit (e.g., Mild, Severe With Psychotic Features, In Partial Remission), as many specifiers (without codes) as apply to the most recent episode (e.g., With Melancholic Features, With Postpartum Onset), and as many specifiers (without codes) as apply to the course of episodes (e.g., With Full Interepisode Recovery); for example, 296.32 Major Depressive Disorder, Recurrent, Moderate, With Atypical Features, With Seasonal Pattern, With Full Interepisode Recovery.

■ 300.4 Dysthymic Disorder

A. Depressed mood for most of the day, for more days than not, as indicated either by subjective account or observation by others, for at least 2 years. **Note:** In children and adolescents, mood can be irritable and duration must be at least 1 year.

B. Presence, while depressed, of two (or more) of the following:

    (1) poor appetite or overeating
    (2) insomnia or hypersomnia
    (3) low energy or fatigue
    (4) low self-esteem
    (5) poor concentration or difficulty making decisions
    (6) feelings of hopelessness

C. During the 2-year period (1 year for children or adolescents) of the disturbance, the person has never been without the symptoms in Criteria A and B for more than 2 months at a time.

D. No Major Depressive Episode (see p. 161) has been present during the first 2 years of the disturbance (1 year for children and adolescents); i.e., the disturbance is not better accounted for by chronic Major Depressive Disorder, or Major Depressive Disorder, In Partial Remission.

    Note: There may have been a previous Major Depressive Episode provided there was a full remission (no significant signs or symptoms for 2 months) before development of the Dysthymic Disorder. In addition, after the initial 2 years (1 year in children or adolescents) of Dysthymic Disorder, there may be superimposed episodes of Major Depressive Disorder, in which case both diagnoses may be given when the criteria are met for a Major Depressive Episode.

E. There has never been a Manic Episode (see p. 163), a Mixed Episode (see p. 165), or a Hypomanic Episode (see p. 165), and criteria have never been met for Cyclothymic Disorder.

F. The disturbance does not occur exclusively during the course of a chronic Psychotic Disorder, such as Schizophrenia or Delusional Disorder.

G. The symptoms are not due to the direct physiological effects of a substance (e.g., a drug of abuse, a medication) or a general medical condition (e.g., hypothyroidism).

H. The symptoms cause clinically significant distress or impairment in social, occupational, or other important areas of functioning.

Specify if:
> **Early Onset:** if onset is before age 21 years
> **Late Onset:** if onset is age 21 years or older

Specify (for most recent 2 years of Dysthymic Disorder):
> **With Atypical Features** (see p. 193)

■ 311 Depressive Disorder Not Otherwise Specified

The Depressive Disorder Not Otherwise Specified category includes disorders with depressive features that do not meet the criteria for Major Depressive Disorder, Dysthymic Disorder, Adjustment Disorder With Depressed Mood (see p. 274), or Adjustment Disorder With Mixed Anxiety and Depressed Mood (see p. 274). Sometimes depressive symptoms can present as part of an Anxiety Disorder Not Otherwise Specified (see p. 217). Examples of Depressive Disorder Not Otherwise Specified include

1. Premenstrual dysphoric disorder: in most menstrual cycles during the past year, symptoms (e.g., markedly

depressed mood, marked anxiety, marked affective lability, decreased interest in activities) regularly occurred during the last week of the luteal phase (and remitted within a few days of the onset of menses). These symptoms must be severe enough to markedly interfere with work, school, or usual activities and be entirely absent for at least 1 week postmenses (see Appendix B in DSM-IV for suggested research criteria).

2. Minor depressive disorder: episodes of at least 2 weeks of depressive symptoms but with fewer than the five items required for Major Depressive Disorder (see Appendix B in DSM-IV for suggested research criteria).

3. Recurrent brief depressive disorder: depressive episodes lasting from 2 days up to 2 weeks, occurring at least once a month for 12 months (not associated with the menstrual cycle) (see Appendix B in DSM-IV for suggested research criteria).

4. Postpsychotic depressive disorder of Schizophrenia: a Major Depressive Episode that occurs during the residual phase of Schizophrenia (see Appendix B in DSM-IV for suggested research criteria).

5. A Major Depressive Episode superimposed on Delusional Disorder, Psychotic Disorder Not Otherwise Specified, or the active phase of Schizophrenia.

6. Situations in which the clinician has concluded that a depressive disorder is present but is unable to determine whether it is primary, due to a general medical condition, or substance induced.

Bipolar Disorders

Bipolar I Disorder

There are six separate criteria sets for Bipolar I Disorder: Single Manic Episode, Most Recent Episode Hypomanic, Most Recent Episode Manic, Most Recent Episode Mixed, Most Recent Episode Depressed, and Most Recent Episode Unspecified. Bipolar I Disorder, Single Manic Episode, is used to describe individuals who are having a first episode of mania. The remaining criteria sets are used to specify the nature of the current (or most recent) episode in individuals who have had recurrent mood episodes.

■ 296.0x   Bipolar I Disorder, Single Manic Episode

A. Presence of only one Manic Episode (see p. 163) and no past Major Depressive Episodes.

Note: Recurrence is defined as either a change in polarity from depression or an interval of at least 2 months without manic symptoms.

B. The Manic Episode is not better accounted for by Schizoaffective Disorder and is not superimposed on Schizophrenia, Schizophreniform Disorder, Delusional Disorder, or Psychotic Disorder Not Otherwise Specified.

Specify if:

Mixed: if symptoms meet criteria for a Mixed Episode (see p. 165)

Specify (for current or most recent episode):
Severity/Psychotic/Remission Specifiers (see p. 189)
With Catatonic Features (see p. 192)
With Postpartum Onset (see p. 194)

Coding note: See p. 179 for recording procedures.

■ 296.40 Bipolar I Disorder, Most Recent Episode Hypomanic

A. Currently (or most recently) in a Hypomanic Episode (see p. 165).

B. There has previously been at least one Manic Episode (see p. 163) or Mixed Episode (see p. 165).

C. The mood symptoms cause clinically significant distress or impairment in social, occupational, or other important areas of functioning.

D. The mood episodes in Criteria A and B are not better accounted for by Schizoaffective Disorder and are not superimposed on Schizophrenia, Schizophreniform Disorder, Delusional Disorder, or Psychotic Disorder Not Otherwise Specified.

Specify:
Longitudinal Course Specifiers (With and Without Interepisode Recovery) (see p. 195)
With Seasonal Pattern (applies only to the pattern of Major Depressive Episodes) (see p. 196)
With Rapid Cycling (see p. 197)

■ 296.4x Bipolar I Disorder, Most Recent Episode Manic

A. Currently (or most recently) in a Manic Episode (see p. 163).

B. There has previously been at least one Major Depressive Episode (see p. 161), Manic Episode (see p. 163), or Mixed Episode (see p. 165).

C. The mood episodes in Criteria A and B are not better accounted for by Schizoaffective Disorder and are not superimposed on Schizophrenia, Schizophreniform Disorder, Delusional Disorder, or Psychotic Disorder Not Otherwise Specified.

Specify (for current or most recent episode):

Severity/Psychotic/Remission Specifiers (see p. 189)
With Catatonic Features (see p. 192)
With Postpartum Onset (see p. 194)

Specify:

Longitudinal Course Specifiers (With and Without Interepisode Recovery) (see p. 195)
With Seasonal Pattern (applies only to the pattern of Major Depressive Episodes) (see p. 196)
With Rapid Cycling (see p. 197)

Coding note: See p. 179 for recording procedures.

■ 296.6x   Bipolar I Disorder, Most Recent Episode Mixed

A. Currently (or most recently) in a Mixed Episode (see p. 165).

B. There has previously been at least one Major Depressive Episode (see p. 161), Manic Episode (see p. 163), or Mixed Episode (see p. 165).

C. The mood episodes in Criteria A and B are not better accounted for by Schizoaffective Disorder and are not superimposed on Schizophrenia, Schizophreniform Disorder, Delusional Disorder, or Psychotic Disorder Not Otherwise Specified.

Specify (for current or most recent episode):
   Severity/Psychotic/Remission Specifiers (see p. 191)
   With Catatonic Features (see p. 192)
   With Postpartum Onset (see p. 194)

Specify:
   Longitudinal Course Specifiers (With and Without Interepisode Recovery) (see p. 195)
   With Seasonal Pattern (applies only to the pattern of Major Depressive Episodes) (see p. 196)
   With Rapid Cycling (see p. 197)

   Coding note: See p. 179 for recording procedures.

■ 296.5x Bipolar I Disorder, Most Recent Episode Depressed

A. Currently (or most recently) in a Major Depressive Episode (see p. 161).

B. There has previously been at least one Manic Episode (see p. 163) or Mixed Episode (see p. 165).

C. The mood episodes in Criteria A and B are not better accounted for by Schizoaffective Disorder and are not superimposed on Schizophrenia, Schizophreniform Disorder, Delusional Disorder, or Psychotic Disorder Not Otherwise Specified.

Specify (for current or most recent episode):
Severity/Psychotic/Remission Specifiers (see p. 187)
Chronic (see p. 192)
With Catatonic Features (see p. 192)
With Melancholic Features (see p. 193)
With Atypical Features (see p. 193)
With Postpartum Onset (see p. 194)

Specify:
Longitudinal Course Specifiers (With and Without Interepisode Recovery) (see p. 195)
With Seasonal Pattern (applies only to the pattern of Major Depressive Episodes) (see p. 196)
With Rapid Cycling (see p. 197)

Coding note: See p. 179 for recording procedures.

■ 296.7 Bipolar I Disorder, Most Recent Episode Unspecified

A. Criteria, except for duration, are currently (or most recently) met for a Manic (see p. 163), a Hypomanic (see p. 165), a Mixed (see p. 165), or a Major Depressive Episode (see p. 161).

B. There has previously been at least one Manic Episode (see p. 163) or Mixed Episode (see p. 165).

C. The mood symptoms cause clinically significant distress or impairment in social, occupational, or other important areas of functioning.

D. The mood symptoms in Criteria A and B are not better accounted for by Schizoaffective Disorder and are not superimposed on Schizophrenia, Schizophreniform Disorder, Delusional Disorder, or Psychotic Disorder Not Otherwise Specified.

E. The mood symptoms in Criteria A and B are not due to the direct physiological effects of a substance (e.g., a drug of abuse, a medication, or other treatment) or a general medical condition (e.g., hyperthyroidism).

Specify:

Longitudinal Course Specifiers (With and Without Interepisode Recovery) (see p. 195)

With Seasonal Pattern (applies only to the pattern of Major Depressive Episodes) (see p. 196)

With Rapid Cycling (see p. 197)

Recording Procedures

The diagnostic codes for Bipolar I Disorder are selected as follows:

1. The first three digits are 296.
2. The fourth digit is 0 if there is a single Manic Episode. For recurrent episodes, the fourth digit is 4 if the current or most recent episode is a Hypomanic Episode or a Manic Episode, 6 if it is a Mixed Episode, 5 if it is a Major Depressive Episode, and 7 if the current or most recent episode is Unspecified.
3. The fifth digit (except for Bipolar I Disorder, Most Recent Episode Hypomanic, and Bipolar I Disorder, Most Recent Episode Unspecified) indicates the following: 1 for Mild severity, 2 for Moderate severity, 3 for Severe Without Psychotic Features, 4 for Severe With Psychotic Features, 5 for In Partial Remission, 6 for In Full Remission, and 0 if Unspecified. Other specifiers for Bipolar I Disorder cannot be coded. For Bipolar I Disorder, Most Recent Episode Hypomanic, the fifth digit is always 0. For Bipolar Disorder, Most Recent Episode Unspecified, there is no fifth digit.

In recording the name of a diagnosis, terms should be listed in the following order: Bipolar I Disorder, specifiers coded in the fourth digit (e.g., Most Recent Episode Manic), specifiers coded in the fifth digit (e.g., Mild, Severe With Psychotic Features, In Partial Remission), as many specifiers (without codes) as apply to the most recent episode (e.g., With Melancholic Features, With Postpartum Onset), and as many specifiers (without codes) as apply to the course of episodes (e.g., With Rapid Cycling); for example, 296.54 Bipolar I Disorder, Most Recent Episode Depressed, Severe

With Psychotic Features, With Melancholic Features, With Rapid Cycling.

Note that if the single episode of Bipolar I Disorder is a Mixed Episode, the diagnosis would be indicated as 296.0x Bipolar I Disorder, Single Manic Episode, Mixed.

■ 296.89 Bipolar II Disorder (Recurrent Major Depressive Episodes With Hypomanic Episodes)

A. Presence (or history) of one or more Major Depressive Episodes (see p. 161).

B. Presence (or history) of at least one Hypomanic Episode (see p. 165).

C. There has never been a Manic Episode (see p. 163) or a Mixed Episode (see p. 165).

D. The mood symptoms in Criteria A and B are not better accounted for by Schizoaffective Disorder and are not superimposed on Schizophrenia, Schizophreniform Disorder, Delusional Disorder, or Psychotic Disorder Not Otherwise Specified.

E. The symptoms cause clinically significant distress or impairment in social, occupational, or other important areas of functioning.

Specify current or most recent episode:
   Hypomanic: if currently (or most recently) in a Hypomanic Episode (see p. 165)
   Depressed: if currently (or most recently) in a Major Depressive Episode (see p. 161)

Specify (for current or most recent Major Depressive Episode only if it is the most recent type of mood episode):

Severity/Psychotic/Remission Specifiers (see p. 187) **Note:** Fifth-digit codes specified on p. 187 cannot be used here because the code for Bipolar II Disorder already uses the fifth digit.

Chronic (see p. 192)

With Catatonic Features (see p. 192)

With Melancholic Features (see p. 193)

With Atypical Features (see p. 193)

With Postpartum Onset (see p. 194)

Specify:

Longitudinal Course Specifiers (With and Without Interepisode Recovery) (see p. 195)

With Seasonal Pattern (applies only to the pattern of Major Depressive Episodes) (see p. 196)

With Rapid Cycling (see p. 197)

■ 301.13 Cyclothymic Disorder

A. For at least 2 years, the presence of numerous periods with hypomanic symptoms (see p. 165) and numerous periods with depressive symptoms that do not meet criteria for a Major Depressive Episode. **Note:** In children and adolescents, the duration must be at least 1 year.

B. During the above 2-year period (1 year in children and adolescents), the person has not been without the symptoms in Criterion A for more than 2 months at a time.

C. No Major Depressive Episode (p. 161), Manic Episode (p. 163), or Mixed Episode (see p. 165) has been present during the first 2 years of the disturbance.

Note: After the initial 2 years (1 year in children and adolescents) of Cyclothymic Disorder, there may be superimposed Manic or Mixed Episodes (in which case both Bipolar I Disorder and Cyclothymic Disorder may be diagnosed) or Major Depressive Episodes (in which case both Bipolar II Disorder and Cyclothymic Disorder may be diagnosed).

D. The symptoms in Criterion A are not better accounted for by Schizoaffective Disorder and are not superimposed on Schizophrenia, Schizophreniform Disorder, Delusional Disorder, or Psychotic Disorder Not Otherwise Specified.

E. The symptoms are not due to the direct physiological effects of a substance (e.g., a drug of abuse, a medication) or a general medical condition (e.g., hyperthyroidism).

F. The symptoms cause clinically significant distress or impairment in social, occupational, or other important areas of functioning.

■ 296.80 Bipolar Disorder Not Otherwise Specified

The Bipolar Disorder Not Otherwise Specified category includes disorders with bipolar features that do not meet criteria for any specific Bipolar Disorder. Examples include

1. Very rapid alternation (over days) between manic symptoms and depressive symptoms that do not meet minimal duration criteria for a Manic Episode or a Major Depressive Episode
2. Recurrent Hypomanic Episodes without intercurrent depressive symptoms
3. A Manic or Mixed Episode superimposed on Delusional

Disorder, residual Schizophrenia, or Psychotic Disorder Not Otherwise Specified

4. Situations in which the clinician has concluded that a Bipolar Disorder is present but is unable to determine whether it is primary, due to a general medical condition, or substance induced

Other Mood Disorders

■ 293.83   Mood Disorder Due to . . .
[*Indicate the General Medical Condition*]

A. A prominent and persistent disturbance in mood predominates in the clinical picture and is characterized by either (or both) of the following:

   (1)   depressed mood or markedly diminished interest or pleasure in all, or almost all, activities
   (2)   elevated, expansive, or irritable mood

B. There is evidence from the history, physical examination, or laboratory findings that the disturbance is the direct physiological consequence of a general medical condition.

C. The disturbance is not better accounted for by another mental disorder (e.g., Adjustment Disorder With Depressed Mood in response to the stress of having a general medical condition).

D. The disturbance does not occur exclusively during the course of a delirium.

E. The symptoms cause clinically significant distress or impairment in social, occupational, or other important areas of functioning.

Specify type:
> **With Depressive Features:** if the predominant mood is depressed but the full criteria are not met for a Major Depressive Episode
>
> **With Major Depressive-Like Episode:** if the full criteria are met (except Criterion D) for a Major Depressive Episode (see p. 161)
>
> **With Manic Features:** if the predominant mood is elevated, euphoric, or irritable
>
> **With Mixed Features:** if the symptoms of both mania and depression are present but neither predominates

Coding note: Include the name of the general medical condition on Axis I, e.g., 293.83 Mood Disorder Due to Hypothyroidism, With Depressive Features; also code the general medical condition on Axis III (see Appendix G for codes).

Coding note: If depressive symptoms occur as part of a preexisting dementia, indicate the depressive symptoms by coding the appropriate subtype of the dementia if one is available, e.g., 290.21 Dementia of the Alzheimer's Type, With Late Onset, With Depressed Mood.

■ Substance-Induced Mood Disorder

A. A prominent and persistent disturbance in mood predominates in the clinical picture and is characterized by either (or both) of the following:

> (1) depressed mood or markedly diminished interest or pleasure in all, or almost all, activities
>
> (2) elevated, expansive, or irritable mood

B. There is evidence from the history, physical examination, or laboratory findings of either (1) or (2):

   (1) the symptoms in Criterion A developed during, or within a month of, Substance Intoxication or Withdrawal

   (2) medication use is etiologically related to the disturbance

C. The disturbance is not better accounted for by a Mood Disorder that is not substance induced. Evidence that the symptoms are better accounted for by a Mood Disorder that is not substance induced might include the following: the symptoms precede the onset of the substance use (or medication use); the symptoms persist for a substantial period of time (e.g., about a month) after the cessation of acute withdrawal or severe intoxication or are substantially in excess of what would be expected given the type or amount of the substance used or the duration of use; or there is other evidence that suggests the existence of an independent non-substance-induced Mood Disorder (e.g., a history of recurrent Major Depressive Episodes).

D. The disturbance does not occur exclusively during the course of a delirium.

E. The symptoms cause clinically significant distress or impairment in social, occupational, or other important areas of functioning.

Note: This diagnosis should be made instead of a diagnosis of Substance Intoxication or Substance Withdrawal only when the mood symptoms are in excess of those usually associated with the intoxication or withdrawal syndrome and when the symptoms are sufficiently severe to warrant independent clinical attention.

Code [Specific Substance]–Induced Mood Disorder:
> (291.89 Alcohol; 292.84 Amphetamine [or Amphetamine-Like Substance]; 292.84 Cocaine; 292.84 Hallucinogen; 292.84 Inhalant; 292.84 Opioid; 292.84 Phencyclidine [or Phencyclidine-Like Substance]; 292.84 Sedative, Hypnotic, or Anxiolytic; 292.84 Other [or Unknown] Substance)

> **Coding note:** For other somatic treatments (e.g., electroconvulsive therapy), the code for "Other Substance" should be used. See p. 115 for recording procedures.

Specify type:
> **With Depressive Features:** if the predominant mood is depressed
> **With Manic Features:** if the predominant mood is elevated, euphoric, or irritable
> **With Mixed Features:** if symptoms of both mania and depression are present and neither predominates

Specify if (see table on p. 106 for applicability by substance):
> **With Onset During Intoxication:** if the criteria are met for Intoxication with the substance and the symptoms develop during the intoxication syndrome
> **With Onset During Withdrawal:** if criteria are met for Withdrawal from the substance and the symptoms develop during, or shortly after, a withdrawal syndrome

■ 296.90   Mood Disorder Not Otherwise Specified

This category includes disorders with mood symptoms that do not meet the criteria for any specific Mood Disorder and in which it is difficult to choose between Depressive Disorder Not Otherwise Specified and Bipolar Disorder Not Otherwise Specified (e.g., acute agitation).

Specifiers Describing Most Recent Episode

The following specifiers pertain to the current (or most recent) mood episode: Severity/Psychotic/Remission, Chronic, With Catatonic Features, With Melancholic Features, With Atypical Features, and With Postpartum Onset. The specifiers that indicate severity, remission, and psychotic features can be coded in the fifth digit of the diagnostic code for most of the Mood Disorders. The other specifiers cannot be coded. Table 1 indicates which episode specifiers apply to each Mood Disorder (see p. 188).

☐ Severity/Psychotic/Remission Specifiers for current (or most recent) Major Depressive Episode

Note: Code in fifth digit. Can be applied to the most recent Major Depressive Episode in Major Depressive Disorder and to a Major Depressive Episode in Bipolar I or II Disorder only if it is the most recent type of mood episode.

.x1—Mild: Few, if any, symptoms in excess of those required to make the diagnosis and symptoms result in only minor impairment in occupational functioning or in usual social activities or relationships with others.

.x2—Moderate: Symptoms or functional impairment between "mild" and "severe."

.x3—Severe Without Psychotic Features: Several symptoms in excess of those required to make the diagnosis, **and** symptoms markedly interfere with occupational functioning or with usual social activities or relationships with others.

.x4—Severe With Psychotic Features: Delusions or hallucinations. If possible, specify whether the psychotic features are mood-congruent or mood-incongruent:

Table 1. Episode specifiers that apply to Mood Disorders

	Severity/ Psychotic/ Remission	Chronic	With Catatonic Features	With Melancholic Features	With Atypical Features	With Postpartum Onset
Major Depressive Disorder, Single Episode	X	X	X	X	X	X
Major Depressive Disorder, Recurrent	X	X	X	X	X	X
Dysthymic Disorder					X	
Bipolar I Disorder, Single Manic Episode	X		X			X
Bipolar I Disorder, Most Recent Episode Hypomanic						
Bipolar I Disorder, Most Recent Episode Manic	X		X			X
Bipolar I Disorder, Most Recent Episode Mixed	X		X			X
Bipolar I Disorder, Most Recent Episode Depressed	X	X	X	X	X	X
Bipolar I Disorder, Most Recent Episode Unspecified						
Bipolar II Disorder, Hypomanic						
Bipolar II Disorder, Depressed	X	X	X	X	X	X
Cyclothymic Disorder						

Mood-Congruent Psychotic Features: Delusions or hallucinations whose content is entirely consistent with the typical depressive themes of personal inadequacy, guilt, disease, death, nihilism, or deserved punishment.

Mood-Incongruent Psychotic Features: Delusions or hallucinations whose content does not involve typical depressive themes of personal inadequacy, guilt, disease, death, nihilism, or deserved punishment. Included are such symptoms as persecutory delusions (not directly related to depressive themes), thought insertion, thought broadcasting, and delusions of control.

.x5—In Partial Remission: Symptoms of a Major Depressive Episode are present but full criteria are not met, or there is a period without any significant symptoms of a Major Depressive Episode lasting less than 2 months following the end of the Major Depressive Episode. (If the Major Depressive Episode was superimposed on Dysthymic Disorder, the diagnosis of Dysthymic Disorder alone is given once the full criteria for a Major Depressive Episode are no longer met.)

.x6—In Full Remission: During the past 2 months, no significant signs or symptoms of the disturbance were present.

.x0—Unspecified.

☐ **Severity/Psychotic/Remission Specifiers for current (or most recent) Manic Episode**

Note: Code in fifth digit. Can be applied to a Manic Episode in Bipolar I Disorder only if it is the most recent type of mood episode.

.x1—Mild: Minimum symptom criteria are met for a Manic Episode.

.x2—Moderate: Extreme increase in activity or impairment in judgment.

.x3—Severe Without Psychotic Features: Almost continual supervision required to prevent physical harm to self or others.

.x4—Severe With Psychotic Features: Delusions or hallucinations. If possible, specify whether the psychotic features are mood-congruent or mood-incongruent:

Mood-Congruent Psychotic Features: Delusions or hallucinations whose content is entirely consistent with the typical manic themes of inflated worth, power, knowledge, identity, or special relationship to a deity or famous person.

Mood-Incongruent Psychotic Features: Delusions or hallucinations whose content does not involve typical manic themes of inflated worth, power, knowledge, identity, or special relationship to a deity or famous person. Included are such symptoms as persecutory delusions (not directly related to grandiose ideas or themes), thought insertion, and delusions of being controlled.

.x5—In Partial Remission: Symptoms of a Manic Episode are present but full criteria are not met, or there is a period without any significant symptoms of a Manic Episode lasting less than 2 months following the end of the Manic Episode.

.x6—In Full Remission: During the past 2 months no significant signs or symptoms of the disturbance were present.

.x0—Unspecified.

☐ Severity/Psychotic/Remission Specifiers for current (or most recent) Mixed Episode

Note: Code in fifth digit. Can be applied to a Mixed Episode in Bipolar I Disorder only if it is the most recent type of mood episode.

.x1—Mild: No more than minimum symptom criteria are met for both a Manic Episode and a Major Depressive Episode.

.x2—Moderate: Symptoms or functional impairment between "mild" and "severe."

.x3—Severe Without Psychotic Features: Almost continual supervision required to prevent physical harm to self or others.

.x4—Severe With Psychotic Features: Delusions or hallucinations. If possible, specify whether the psychotic features are mood-congruent or mood-incongruent:

> **Mood-Congruent Psychotic Features:**   Delusions or hallucinations whose content is entirely consistent with the typical manic or depressive themes.
>
> **Mood-Incongruent Psychotic Features:**   Delusions or hallucinations whose content does not involve typical manic or depressive themes. Included are such symptoms as persecutory delusions (not directly related to grandiose or depressive themes), thought insertion, and delusions of being controlled.

.x5—In Partial Remission: Symptoms of a Mixed Episode are present but full criteria are not met, or there is a period without any significant symptoms of a Mixed Episode lasting less than 2 months following the end of the Mixed Episode.

.x6—In Full Remission: During the past 2 months, no significant signs or symptoms of the disturbance were present.

.x0—Unspecified.

☐ Chronic Specifier

Specify if:

Chronic (can be applied to the current or most recent Major Depressive Episode in Major Depressive Disorder and to a Major Depressive Episode in Bipolar I or II Disorder only if it is the most recent type of mood episode)

Full criteria for a Major Depressive Episode have been met continuously for at least the past 2 years.

☐ Catatonic Features Specifier

Specify if:

With Catatonic Features (can be applied to the current or most recent Major Depressive Episode, Manic Episode, or Mixed Episode in Major Depressive Disorder, Bipolar I Disorder, or Bipolar II Disorder)

The clinical picture is dominated by at least two of the following:

(1)   motoric immobility as evidenced by catalepsy (including waxy flexibility) or stupor

(2)   excessive motor activity (that is apparently purposeless and not influenced by external stimuli)

(3)   extreme negativism (an apparently motiveless resistance to all instructions or maintenance of a rigid posture against attempts to be moved) or mutism

(4)   peculiarities of voluntary movement as evidenced by posturing (voluntary assumption of inappropriate or bizarre postures), stereotyped movements, prominent mannerisms, or prominent grimacing

(5)   echolalia or echopraxia

☐ Melancholic Features Specifier

Specify if:

With Melancholic Features (can be applied to the current or most recent Major Depressive Episode in Major Depressive Disorder and to a Major Depressive Episode in Bipolar I or Bipolar II Disorder only if it is the most recent type of mood episode)

A. Either of the following, occurring during the most severe period of the current episode:

  (1)   loss of pleasure in all, or almost all, activities
  (2)   lack of reactivity to usually pleasurable stimuli (does not feel much better, even temporarily, when something good happens)

B. Three (or more) of the following:

  (1)   distinct quality of depressed mood (i.e., the depressed mood is experienced as distinctly different from the kind of feeling experienced after the death of a loved one)
  (2)   depression regularly worse in the morning
  (3)   early morning awakening (at least 2 hours before usual time of awakening)
  (4)   marked psychomotor retardation or agitation
  (5)   significant anorexia or weight loss
  (6)   excessive or inappropriate guilt

☐ Atypical Features Specifier

Specify if:

With Atypical Features (can be applied when these features predominate during the most recent 2 weeks of a Major Depressive Episode in Major Depressive Disorder or in Bipolar I or Bipolar II Disorder when the Major Depressive Episode is the most recent type of mood episode, or when these features predominate during the most recent 2 years of Dysthymic Disorder)

A. Mood reactivity (i.e., mood brightens in response to actual or potential positive events)

B. Two (or more) of the following features:
    (1) significant weight gain or increase in appetite
    (2) hypersomnia
    (3) leaden paralysis (i.e., heavy, leaden feelings in arms or legs)
    (4) long-standing pattern of interpersonal rejection sensitivity (not limited to episodes of mood disturbance) that results in significant social or occupational impairment

C. Criteria are not met for With Melancholic Features or With Catatonic Features during the same episode.

☐ **Postpartum Onset Specifier**

Specify if:
   With Postpartum Onset (can be applied to the current or most recent Major Depressive, Manic, or Mixed Episode in Major Depressive Disorder, Bipolar I Disorder, or Bipolar II Disorder; or to Brief Psychotic Disorder)

Onset of episode within 4 weeks postpartum

Specifiers Describing Course of Recurrent Episodes

Specifiers that describe the course of recurrent episodes include Longitudinal Course Specifiers (With or Without Full Interepisode Recovery), Seasonal Pattern, and Rapid Cycling. These specifiers cannot be coded. Table 2 indicates which course specifiers apply to each Mood Disorder (see p. 198).

☐ **Longitudinal Course Specifiers**

Specify if (can be applied to Recurrent Major Depressive Disorder or Bipolar I or II Disorder):

   With Full Interepisode Recovery: if full remission is attained between the two most recent Mood Episodes

   Without Full Interepisode Recovery: if full remission is not attained between the two most recent Mood Episodes

The four graphs below depict prototypical courses:

A. Recurrent, with full interepisode recovery, with no Dysthymic Disorder

B. Recurrent, without full interepisode recovery, with no Dysthymic Disorder

C. Recurrent, with full interepisode recovery, super-imposed on Dysthymic Disorder (also code 300.4)

D. Recurrent, without full interepisode recovery, super-imposed on Dysthymic Disorder (also code 300.4)

☐ Seasonal Pattern Specifier

Specify if:

With Seasonal Pattern (can be applied to the pattern of Major Depressive Episodes in Bipolar I Disorder, Bipolar II Disorder, or Major Depressive Disorder, Recurrent)

A. There has been a regular temporal relationship between the onset of Major Depressive Episodes in Bipolar I or Bipolar II Disorder or Major Depressive Disorder, Recurrent, and a particular time of the year (e.g., regular appearance of the Major Depressive Episode in the fall or winter).

Note: Do not include cases in which there is an obvious effect of seasonal-related psychosocial stressors (e.g., regularly being unemployed every winter).

B. Full remissions (or a change from depression to mania or hypomania) also occur at a characteristic time of the year (e.g., depression disappears in the spring).

C. In the last 2 years, two Major Depressive Episodes have occurred that demonstrate the temporal seasonal relationships defined in Criteria A and B, and no nonseasonal Major Depressive Episodes have occurred during that same period.

D. Seasonal Major Depressive Episodes (as described above) substantially outnumber the nonseasonal Major Depressive Episodes that may have occurred over the individual's lifetime.

☐ Rapid-Cycling Specifier

Specify if:

With Rapid Cycling (can be applied to Bipolar I Disorder or Bipolar II Disorder)

At least four episodes of a mood disturbance in the previous 12 months that meet criteria for a Major Depressive, Manic, Mixed, or Hypomanic Episode.

Note: Episodes are demarcated either by partial or full remission for at least 2 months or a switch to an episode of opposite polarity (e.g., Major Depressive Episode to Manic Episode).

Table 2. Course specifiers that apply to Mood Disorders

	With/Without Interepisode Recovery	Seasonal Pattern	Rapid Cycling
Major Depressive Disorder, Single Episode			
Major Depressive Disorder, Recurrent	X	X	
Dysthymic Disorder			
Bipolar I Disorder, Single Manic Episode			
Bipolar I Disorder, Most Recent Episode Hypomanic	X	X	X
Bipolar I Disorder, Most Recent Episode Manic	X	X	X
Bipolar I Disorder, Most Recent Episode Mixed	X	X	X
Bipolar I Disorder, Most Recent Episode Depressed	X	X	X
Bipolar I Disorder, Most Recent Episode Unspecified	X	X	X
Bipolar II Disorder, Hypomanic	X	X	X
Bipolar II Disorder, Depressed	X	X	X
Cyclothymic Disorder			

Anxiety Disorders

Because Panic Attacks and Agoraphobia occur in the context of several disorders in this section, criteria sets for a Panic Attack and for Agoraphobia are listed separately at the beginning. They do not, however, have their own diagnostic codes and cannot be diagnosed as separate entities.

☐ Panic Attack

Note: A Panic Attack is not a codable disorder. Code the specific diagnosis in which the Panic Attack occurs (e.g., 300.21 Panic Disorder With Agoraphobia [p. 202]).

A discrete period of intense fear or discomfort, in which four (or more) of the following symptoms developed abruptly and reached a peak within 10 minutes:

(1) palpitations, pounding heart, or accelerated heart rate
(2) sweating
(3) trembling or shaking
(4) sensations of shortness of breath or smothering
(5) feeling of choking
(6) chest pain or discomfort
(7) nausea or abdominal distress
(8) feeling dizzy, unsteady, lightheaded, or faint
(9) derealization (feelings of unreality) or depersonalization (being detached from oneself)
(10) fear of losing control or going crazy
(11) fear of dying

(12)   paresthesias (numbness or tingling sensations)
(13)   chills or hot flushes

☐ **Agoraphobia**

Note: Agoraphobia is not a codable disorder. Code the specific disorder in which the Agoraphobia occurs (e.g., 300.21 Panic Disorder With Agoraphobia [p. 202] or 300.22 Agoraphobia Without History of Panic Disorder [p. 203]).

A.   Anxiety about being in places or situations from which escape might be difficult (or embarrassing) or in which help may not be available in the event of having an unexpected or situationally predisposed Panic Attack or panic-like symptoms. Agoraphobic fears typically involve characteristic clusters of situations that include being outside the home alone; being in a crowd or standing in a line; being on a bridge; and traveling in a bus, train, or automobile.

Note: Consider the diagnosis of Specific Phobia if the avoidance is limited to one or only a few specific situations, or Social Phobia if the avoidance is limited to social situations.

B.   The situations are avoided (e.g., travel is restricted) or else are endured with marked distress or with anxiety about having a Panic Attack or panic-like symptoms, or require the presence of a companion.

C.   The anxiety or phobic avoidance is not better accounted for by another mental disorder, such as Social Phobia (e.g., avoidance limited to social situations because of fear of embarrassment), Specific Phobia (e.g., avoidance limited to a single situation like elevators), Obsessive-Compulsive Disorder (e.g., avoidance of dirt in someone with an obsession about contamination), Posttraumatic

Stress Disorder (e.g., avoidance of stimuli associated with a severe stressor), or Separation Anxiety Disorder (e.g., avoidance of leaving home or relatives).

■ 300.01 Panic Disorder Without Agoraphobia

A. Both (1) and (2):

    (1) recurrent unexpected Panic Attacks (see p. 199)

    (2) at least one of the attacks has been followed by 1 month (or more) of one (or more) of the following:

        (a) persistent concern about having additional attacks

        (b) worry about the implications of the attack or its consequences (e.g., losing control, having a heart attack, "going crazy")

        (c) a significant change in behavior related to the attacks

B. Absence of Agoraphobia (see p. 200).

C. The Panic Attacks are not due to the direct physiological effects of a substance (e.g., a drug of abuse, a medication) or a general medical condition (e.g., hyperthyroidism).

D. The Panic Attacks are not better accounted for by another mental disorder, such as Social Phobia (e.g., occurring on exposure to feared social situations), Specific Phobia (e.g., on exposure to a specific phobic situation), Obsessive-Compulsive Disorder (e.g., on exposure to dirt in someone with an obsession about contamination), Posttraumatic Stress Disorder (e.g., in response to stimuli associated with a severe stressor), or

Separation Anxiety Disorder (e.g., in response to being away from home or close relatives).

■ 300.21 Panic Disorder With Agoraphobia

A. Both (1) and (2):

    (1)   recurrent unexpected Panic Attacks (see p. 199)

    (2)   at least one of the attacks has been followed by 1 month (or more) of one (or more) of the following:

        (a)   persistent concern about having additional attacks

        (b)   worry about the implications of the attack or its consequences (e.g., losing control, having a heart attack, "going crazy")

        (c)   a significant change in behavior related to the attacks

B. The presence of Agoraphobia (see p. 200).

C. The Panic Attacks are not due to the direct physiological effects of a substance (e.g., a drug of abuse, a medication) or a general medical condition (e.g., hyperthyroidism).

D. The Panic Attacks are not better accounted for by another mental disorder, such as Social Phobia (e.g., occurring on exposure to feared social situations), Specific Phobia (e.g., on exposure to a specific phobic situation), Obsessive-Compulsive Disorder (e.g., on exposure to dirt in someone with an obsession about contamination), Posttraumatic Stress Disorder (e.g., in response to stimuli associated with a severe stressor), or Separation Anxiety Disorder (e.g., in response to being away from home or close relatives).

■ 300.22 Agoraphobia Without History of Panic Disorder

A. The presence of Agoraphobia (see p. 200) related to fear of developing panic-like symptoms (e.g., dizziness or diarrhea).

B. Criteria have never been met for Panic Disorder (see p. 202).

C. The disturbance is not due to the direct physiological effects of a substance (e.g., a drug of abuse, a medication) or a general medical condition.

D. If an associated general medical condition is present, the fear described in Criterion A is clearly in excess of that usually associated with the condition.

■ 300.29 Specific Phobia (*formerly* Simple Phobia)

A. Marked and persistent fear that is excessive or unreasonable, cued by the presence or anticipation of a specific object or situation (e.g., flying, heights, animals, receiving an injection, seeing blood).

B. Exposure to the phobic stimulus almost invariably provokes an immediate anxiety response, which may take the form of a situationally bound or situationally predisposed Panic Attack. **Note:** In children, the anxiety may be expressed by crying, tantrums, freezing, or clinging.

C. The person recognizes that the fear is excessive or unreasonable. **Note:** In children, this feature may be absent.

D. The phobic situation(s) is avoided or else is endured with intense anxiety or distress.

E. The avoidance, anxious anticipation, or distress in the feared situation(s) interferes significantly with the person's normal routine, occupational (or academic) functioning, or social activities or relationships, or there is marked distress about having the phobia.

F. In individuals under age 18 years, the duration is at least 6 months.

G. The anxiety, Panic Attacks, or phobic avoidance associated with the specific object or situation are not better accounted for by another mental disorder, such as Obsessive-Compulsive Disorder (e.g., fear of dirt in someone with an obsession about contamination), Post-traumatic Stress Disorder (e.g., avoidance of stimuli associated with a severe stressor), Separation Anxiety Disorder (e.g., avoidance of school), Social Phobia (e.g., avoidance of social situations because of fear of embarrassment), Panic Disorder With Agoraphobia, or Agoraphobia Without History of Panic Disorder.

Specify type:
    Animal Type: if the fear is cued by animals or insects. This subtype generally has a childhood onset.
    Natural Environment Type: if the fear is cued by objects in the natural environment, such as storms, heights, or water. This subtype generally has a childhood onset.
    Blood-Injection-Injury Type: if the fear is cued by seeing blood or an injury or by receiving an injection or other invasive medical procedure. This subtype is

highly familial and is often characterized by a strong
vasovagal response.

Situational Type: if the fear is cued by a specific
situation such as public transportation, tunnels, brid-
ges, elevators, flying, driving, or enclosed places. This
subtype has a bimodal age-at-onset distribution, with
one peak in childhood and another peak in the
mid-20s. This subtype appears to be similar to Panic
Disorder With Agoraphobia in its characteristic sex
ratios, familial aggregation pattern, and age at onset.

Other Type: if the fear is cued by other stimuli. These
stimuli might include the fear or avoidance of situations that might lead to choking, vomiting, or con-
tracting an illness; "space" phobia (i.e., the individual
is afraid of falling down if away from walls or other
means of physical support); and children's fears of
loud sounds or costumed characters.

■ 300.23 Social Phobia (Social Anxiety Disorder)

A. A marked and persistent fear of one or more social or
performance situations in which the person is exposed
to unfamiliar people or to possible scrutiny by others.
The individual fears that he or she will act in a way (or
show anxiety symptoms) that will be humiliating or
embarrassing. **Note:** In children, there must be evidence of the capacity for age-appropriate social relationships with familiar people and the anxiety must occur
in peer settings, not just in interactions with adults.

B. Exposure to the feared social situation almost invariably
provokes anxiety, which may take the form of a situationally bound or situationally predisposed Panic Attack.

Note: In children, the anxiety may be expressed by crying, tantrums, freezing, or shrinking from social situations with unfamiliar people.

C. The person recognizes that the fear is excessive or unreasonable. **Note:** In children, this feature may be absent.

D. The feared social or performance situations are avoided or else are endured with intense anxiety or distress.

E. The avoidance, anxious anticipation, or distress in the feared social or performance situation(s) interferes significantly with the person's normal routine, occupational (academic) functioning, or social activities or relationships, or there is marked distress about having the phobia.

F. In individuals under age 18 years, the duration is at least 6 months.

G. The fear or avoidance is not due to the direct physiological effects of a substance (e.g., a drug of abuse, a medication) or a general medical condition and is not better accounted for by another mental disorder (e.g., Panic Disorder With or Without Agoraphobia, Separation Anxiety Disorder, Body Dysmorphic Disorder, a Pervasive Developmental Disorder, or Schizoid Personality Disorder).

H. If a general medical condition or another mental disorder is present, the fear in Criterion A is unrelated to it, e.g., the fear is not of Stuttering, trembling in Parkinson's disease, or exhibiting abnormal eating behavior in Anorexia Nervosa or Bulimia Nervosa.

Specify if:

Generalized: if the fears include most social situations (e.g., initiating or maintaining conversations, participating in small groups, dating, speaking to authority figures, attending parties). **Note:** Also consider the additional diagnosis of Avoidant Personality Disorder.

■ 300.3 Obsessive-Compulsive Disorder

A. Either obsessions or compulsions:

Obsessions as defined by (1), (2), (3), and (4):

(1) recurrent and persistent thoughts, impulses, or images that are experienced, at some time during the disturbance, as intrusive and inappropriate and that cause marked anxiety or distress

(2) the thoughts, impulses, or images are not simply excessive worries about real-life problems

(3) the person attempts to ignore or suppress such thoughts, impulses, or images, or to neutralize them with some other thought or action

(4) the person recognizes that the obsessional thoughts, impulses, or images are a product of his or her own mind (not imposed from without as in thought insertion)

Compulsions as defined by (1) and (2):

(1) repetitive behaviors (e.g., hand washing, ordering, checking) or mental acts (e.g., praying, counting, repeating words silently) that the person feels driven to perform in response to an obsession, or according to rules that must be applied rigidly

   (2)   the behaviors or mental acts are aimed at prevent-
         ing or reducing distress or preventing some
         dreaded event or situation; however, these behav-
         iors or mental acts either are not connected in a
         realistic way with what they are designed to neu-
         tralize or prevent or are clearly excessive

B. At some point during the course of the disorder, the
    person has recognized that the obsessions or compul-
    sions are excessive or unreasonable. **Note:** This does
    not apply to children.

C. The obsessions or compulsions cause marked distress,
    are time consuming (take more than 1 hour a day), or
    significantly interfere with the person's normal routine,
    occupational (or academic) functioning, or usual social
    activities or relationships.

D. If another Axis I disorder is present, the content of the
    obsessions or compulsions is not restricted to it (e.g.,
    preoccupation with food in the presence of an Eating
    Disorder; hair pulling in the presence of Trichotillo-
    mania; concern with appearance in the presence of
    Body Dysmorphic Disorder; preoccupation with drugs
    in the presence of a Substance Use Disorder; preoccu-
    pation with having a serious illness in the presence of
    Hypochondriasis; preoccupation with sexual urges or
    fantasies in the presence of a Paraphilia; or guilty rumi-
    nations in the presence of Major Depressive Disorder).

E. The disturbance is not due to the direct physiological
    effects of a substance (e.g., a drug of abuse, a medica-
    tion) or a general medical condition.

Specify if:

> **With Poor Insight:**   if, for most of the time during the current episode, the person does not recognize that the obsessions and compulsions are excessive or unreasonable

■ 309.81   Posttraumatic Stress Disorder

A. The person has been exposed to a traumatic event in which both of the following were present:

  (1) the person experienced, witnessed, or was confronted with an event or events that involved actual or threatened death or serious injury, or a threat to the physical integrity of self or others

  (2) the person's response involved intense fear, help-lessness, or horror.   **Note:** In children, this may be expressed instead by disorganized or agitated behavior

B. The traumatic event is persistently reexperienced in one (or more) of the following ways:

  (1) recurrent and intrusive distressing recollections of the event, including images, thoughts, or perceptions.   **Note:** In young children, repetitive play may occur in which themes or aspects of the trauma are expressed.

  (2) recurrent distressing dreams of the event.   **Note:** In children, there may be frightening dreams without recognizable content.

  (3) acting or feeling as if the traumatic event were recurring (includes a sense of reliving the experience, illusions, hallucinations, and dissociative flashback episodes, including those that occur on awakening or when intoxicated).   **Note:** In young children, trauma-specific reenactment may occur.

(4) intense psychological distress at exposure to internal or external cues that symbolize or resemble an aspect of the traumatic event

(5) physiological reactivity on exposure to internal or external cues that symbolize or resemble an aspect of the traumatic event

C. Persistent avoidance of stimuli associated with the trauma and numbing of general responsiveness (not present before the trauma), as indicated by three (or more) of the following:

(1) efforts to avoid thoughts, feelings, or conversations associated with the trauma

(2) efforts to avoid activities, places, or people that arouse recollections of the trauma

(3) inability to recall an important aspect of the trauma

(4) markedly diminished interest or participation in significant activities

(5) feeling of detachment or estrangement from others

(6) restricted range of affect (e.g., unable to have loving feelings)

(7) sense of a foreshortened future (e.g., does not expect to have a career, marriage, children, or a normal life span)

D. Persistent symptoms of increased arousal (not present before the trauma), as indicated by two (or more) of the following:

(1) difficulty falling or staying asleep

(2) irritability or outbursts of anger

(3) difficulty concentrating

(4) hypervigilance

(5) exaggerated startle response

E. Duration of the disturbance (symptoms in Criteria B, C, and D) is more than 1 month.

F. The disturbance causes clinically significant distress or impairment in social, occupational, or other important areas of functioning.

Specify if:
    Acute: if duration of symptoms is less than 3 months
    Chronic: if duration of symptoms is 3 months or more

Specify if:
    With Delayed Onset: if onset of symptoms is at least 6 months after the stressor

■ 308.3 Acute Stress Disorder

A. The person has been exposed to a traumatic event in which both of the following were present:

    (1) the person experienced, witnessed, or was confronted with an event or events that involved actual or threatened death or serious injury, or a threat to the physical integrity of self or others

    (2) the person's response involved intense fear, helplessness, or horror

B. Either while experiencing or after experiencing the distressing event, the individual has three (or more) of the following dissociative symptoms:

    (1) a subjective sense of numbing, detachment, or absence of emotional responsiveness

    (2) a reduction in awareness of his or her surroundings (e.g., "being in a daze")

    (3) derealization

    (4) depersonalization

(5)   dissociative amnesia (i.e., inability to recall an important aspect of the trauma)

C.   The traumatic event is persistently reexperienced in at least one of the following ways: recurrent images, thoughts, dreams, illusions, flashback episodes, or a sense of reliving the experience; or distress on exposure to reminders of the traumatic event.

D.   Marked avoidance of stimuli that arouse recollections of the trauma (e.g., thoughts, feelings, conversations, activities, places, people).

E.   Marked symptoms of anxiety or increased arousal (e.g., difficulty sleeping, irritability, poor concentration, hypervigilance, exaggerated startle response, motor restlessness).

F.   The disturbance causes clinically significant distress or impairment in social, occupational, or other important areas of functioning or impairs the individual's ability to pursue some necessary task, such as obtaining necessary assistance or mobilizing personal resources by telling family members about the traumatic experience.

G.   The disturbance lasts for a minimum of 2 days and a maximum of 4 weeks and occurs within 4 weeks of the traumatic event.

H.   The disturbance is not due to the direct physiological effects of a substance (e.g., a drug of abuse, a medication) or a general medical condition, is not better accounted for by Brief Psychotic Disorder, and is not merely an exacerbation of a preexisting Axis I or Axis II disorder.

■ 300.02 Generalized Anxiety Disorder (Includes Overanxious Disorder of Childhood)

A. Excessive anxiety and worry (apprehensive expectation), occurring more days than not for at least 6 months, about a number of events or activities (such as work or school performance).

B. The person finds it difficult to control the worry.

C. The anxiety and worry are associated with three (or more) of the following six symptoms (with at least some symptoms present for more days than not for the past 6 months). **Note:** Only one item is required in children.

   (1) restlessness or feeling keyed up or on edge
   (2) being easily fatigued
   (3) difficulty concentrating or mind going blank
   (4) irritability
   (5) muscle tension
   (6) sleep disturbance (difficulty falling or staying asleep, or restless unsatisfying sleep)

D. The focus of the anxiety and worry is not confined to features of an Axis I disorder, e.g., the anxiety or worry is not about having a Panic Attack (as in Panic Disorder), being embarrassed in public (as in Social Phobia), being contaminated (as in Obsessive-Compulsive Disorder), being away from home or close relatives (as in Separation Anxiety Disorder), gaining weight (as in Anorexia Nervosa), having multiple physical complaints (as in Somatization Disorder), or having a serious illness (as in Hypochondriasis), and the anxiety and worry do not occur exclusively during Posttraumatic Stress Disorder.

E. The anxiety, worry, or physical symptoms cause clinically significant distress or impairment in social, occupational, or other important areas of functioning.

F. The disturbance is not due to the direct physiological effects of a substance (e.g., a drug of abuse, a medication) or a general medical condition (e.g., hyperthyroidism) and does not occur exclusively during a Mood Disorder, a Psychotic Disorder, or a Pervasive Developmental Disorder.

■ 293.84 Anxiety Disorder Due to . . . [*Indicate the General Medical Condition*]

A. Prominent anxiety, Panic Attacks, or obsessions or compulsions predominate in the clinical picture.

B. There is evidence from the history, physical examination, or laboratory findings that the disturbance is the direct physiological consequence of a general medical condition.

C. The disturbance is not better accounted for by another mental disorder (e.g., Adjustment Disorder With Anxiety in which the stressor is a serious general medical condition).

D. The disturbance does not occur exclusively during the course of a delirium.

E. The disturbance causes clinically significant distress or impairment in social, occupational, or other important areas of functioning.

Specify if:

> **With Generalized Anxiety:** if excessive anxiety or worry about a number of events or activities predominates in the clinical presentation
>
> **With Panic Attacks:** if Panic Attacks (see p. 199) predominate in the clinical presentation
>
> **With Obsessive-Compulsive Symptoms:** if obsessions or compulsions predominate in the clinical presentation

Coding note: Include the name of the general medical condition on Axis I, e.g., 293.89 Anxiety Disorder Due to Pheochromocytoma, With Generalized Anxiety; also code the general medical condition on Axis III (see Appendix G for codes).

■ Substance-Induced Anxiety Disorder

A. Prominent anxiety, Panic Attacks, or obsessions or compulsions predominate in the clinical picture.

B. There is evidence from the history, physical examination, or laboratory findings of either (1) or (2):

   (1) the symptoms in Criterion A developed during, or within 1 month of, Substance Intoxication or Withdrawal

   (2) medication use is etiologically related to the disturbance

C. The disturbance is not better accounted for by an Anxiety Disorder that is not substance induced. Evidence that the symptoms are better accounted for by an Anxiety Disorder that is not substance induced might include the following: the symptoms precede the onset of the substance use (or medication use); the symptoms persist for a substantial period of time (e.g., about a month) after the cessation of acute withdrawal or severe intoxication or are substantially in excess of what would be expected given the type or amount of the substance used or the duration of use; or there is other evidence suggesting the existence of an independent non-substance-induced Anxiety Disorder (e.g., a history of recurrent non-substance-related episodes).

D. The disturbance does not occur exclusively during the course of a delirium.

E. The disturbance causes clinically significant distress or impairment in social, occupational, or other important areas of functioning.

Note: This diagnosis should be made instead of a diagnosis of Substance Intoxication or Substance Withdrawal only when the anxiety symptoms are in excess of those usually associated with the intoxication or withdrawal syndrome and when the anxiety symptoms are sufficiently severe to warrant independent clinical attention.

Code [Specific Substance]–Induced Anxiety Disorder
(291.89 Alcohol; 292.89 Amphetamine (or Amphetamine-Like Substance); 292.89 Caffeine; 292.89 Cannabis; 292.89 Cocaine; 292.89 Hallucinogen; 292.89 Inhalant; 292.89 Phencyclidine (or Phencyclidine-Like Substance); 292.89 Sedative, Hypnotic, or Anxiolytic; 292.89 Other [or Unknown] Substance)

Coding note: See p. 115 for recording procedures.

Specify if:
With Generalized Anxiety: if excessive anxiety or worry about a number of events or activities predominates in the clinical presentation
With Panic Attacks: if Panic Attacks (see p. 199) predominate in the clinical presentation

With Obsessive-Compulsive Symptoms: if obsessions or compulsions predominate in the clinical presentation

With Phobic Symptoms: if phobic symptoms predominate in the clinical presentation

Specify if (see table on p. 106 for applicability by substance):

With Onset During Intoxication: if the criteria are met for Intoxication with the substance and the symptoms develop during the intoxication syndrome

With Onset During Withdrawal: if criteria are met for Withdrawal from the substance and the symptoms develop during, or shortly after, a withdrawal syndrome

■ 300.00   Anxiety Disorder Not Otherwise Specified

This category includes disorders with prominent anxiety or phobic avoidance that do not meet criteria for any specific Anxiety Disorder, Adjustment Disorder With Anxiety, or Adjustment Disorder With Mixed Anxiety and Depressed Mood. Examples include

1. Mixed anxiety-depressive disorder: clinically significant symptoms of anxiety and depression, but the criteria are not met for either a specific Mood Disorder or a specific Anxiety Disorder (see Appendix B in DSM-IV for suggested research criteria)
2. Clinically significant social phobic symptoms that are related to the social impact of having a general medical condition or mental disorder (e.g., Parkinson's disease, dermatological conditions, Stuttering, Anorexia Nervosa, Body Dysmorphic Disorder)

3. Situations in which the clinician has concluded that an Anxiety Disorder is present but is unable to determine whether it is primary, due to a general medical condition, or substance induced

Somatoform Disorders

■ 300.81   Somatization Disorder

A.   A history of many physical complaints beginning before age 30 years that occur over a period of several years and result in treatment being sought or significant impairment in social, occupational, or other important areas of functioning.

B.   Each of the following criteria must have been met, with individual symptoms occurring at any time during the course of the disturbance:

   (1)   *four pain symptoms:*   a history of pain related to at least four different sites or functions (e.g., head, abdomen, back, joints, extremities, chest, rectum, during menstruation, during sexual intercourse, or during urination)

   (2)   *two gastrointestinal symptoms:*   a history of at least two gastrointestinal symptoms other than pain (e.g., nausea, bloating, vomiting other than during pregnancy, diarrhea, or intolerance of several different foods)

   (3)   *one sexual symptom:*   a history of at least one sexual or reproductive symptom other than pain (e.g., sexual indifference, erectile or ejaculatory dysfunction, irregular menses, excessive menstrual bleeding, vomiting throughout pregnancy)

(4) *one pseudoneurological symptom:* a history of at least one symptom or deficit suggesting a neurological condition not limited to pain (conversion symptoms such as impaired coordination or balance, paralysis or localized weakness, difficulty swallowing or lump in throat, aphonia, urinary retention, hallucinations, loss of touch or pain sensation, double vision, blindness, deafness, seizures; dissociative symptoms such as amnesia; or loss of consciousness other than fainting)

C. Either (1) or (2):

(1) after appropriate investigation, each of the symptoms in Criterion B cannot be fully explained by a known general medical condition or the direct effects of a substance (e.g., a drug of abuse, a medication)

(2) when there is a related general medical condition, the physical complaints or resulting social or occupational impairment are in excess of what would be expected from the history, physical examination, or laboratory findings

D. The symptoms are not intentionally produced or feigned (as in Factitious Disorder or Malingering).

■ 300.82 Undifferentiated Somatoform Disorder

A. One or more physical complaints (e.g., fatigue, loss of appetite, gastrointestinal or urinary complaints).

B. Either (1) or (2):

    (1)   after appropriate investigation, the symptoms cannot be fully explained by a known general medical condition or the direct effects of a substance (e.g., a drug of abuse, a medication)

    (2)   when there is a related general medical condition, the physical complaints or resulting social or occupational impairment is in excess of what would be expected from the history, physical examination, or laboratory findings

C. The symptoms cause clinically significant distress or impairment in social, occupational, or other important areas of functioning.

D. The duration of the disturbance is at least 6 months.

E. The disturbance is not better accounted for by another mental disorder (e.g., another Somatoform Disorder, Sexual Dysfunction, Mood Disorder, Anxiety Disorder, Sleep Disorder, or Psychotic Disorder).

F. The symptom is not intentionally produced or feigned (as in Factitious Disorder or Malingering).

■ 300.11 Conversion Disorder

A. One or more symptoms or deficits affecting voluntary motor or sensory function that suggest a neurological or other general medical condition.

B. Psychological factors are judged to be associated with the symptom or deficit because the initiation or exacerbation of the symptom or deficit is preceded by conflicts or other stressors.

C. The symptom or deficit is not intentionally produced or feigned (as in Factitious Disorder or Malingering).

D. The symptom or deficit cannot, after appropriate investigation, be fully explained by a general medical condition, or by the direct effects of a substance, or as a culturally sanctioned behavior or experience.

E. The symptom or deficit causes clinically significant distress or impairment in social, occupational, or other important areas of functioning or warrants medical evaluation.

F. The symptom or deficit is not limited to pain or sexual dysfunction, does not occur exclusively during the course of Somatization Disorder, and is not better accounted for by another mental disorder.

Specify type of symptom or deficit:

With Motor Symptom or Deficit (e.g., impaired coordination or balance, paralysis or localized weakness, difficulty swallowing or "lump in throat," aphonia, and urinary retention)

With Sensory Symptom or Deficit (e.g., loss of touch or pain sensation, double vision, blindness, deafness, and hallucinations)

With Seizures or Convulsions: includes seizures or convulsions with voluntary motor or sensory components

With Mixed Presentation: if symptoms of more than one category are evident

■ Pain Disorder

A. Pain in one or more anatomical sites is the predominant focus of the clinical presentation and is of sufficient severity to warrant clinical attention.

B. The pain causes clinically significant distress or impairment in social, occupational, or other important areas of functioning.

C. Psychological factors are judged to have an important role in the onset, severity, exacerbation, or maintenance of the pain.

D. The symptom or deficit is not intentionally produced or feigned (as in Factitious Disorder or Malingering).

E. The pain is not better accounted for by a Mood, Anxiety, or Psychotic Disorder and does not meet criteria for Dyspareunia.

Code as follows:
> **307.80 Pain Disorder Associated With Psychological Factors:** psychological factors are judged to have the major role in the onset, severity, exacerbation, or maintenance of the pain. (If a general medical condition is present, it does not have a major role in the onset, severity, exacerbation, or maintenance of the pain.) This type of Pain Disorder is not diagnosed if criteria are also met for Somatization Disorder.

Specify if:
> **Acute:** duration of less than 6 months
> **Chronic:** duration of 6 months or longer

307.89 Pain Disorder Associated With Both Psychological Factors and a General Medical Condition: both psychological factors and a general medical condition are judged to have important roles in the onset, severity, exacerbation, or maintenance of the pain. The associated general medical condition or anatomical site of the pain (see below) is coded on Axis III.

Specify if:
    Acute: duration of less than 6 months
    Chronic: duration of 6 months or longer

Note: The following is not considered to be a mental disorder and is included here to facilitate differential diagnosis.

Pain Disorder Associated With a General Medical Condition: a general medical condition has a major role in the onset, severity, exacerbation, or maintenance of the pain. (If psychological factors are present, they are not judged to have a major role in the onset, severity, exacerbation, or maintenance of the pain.) The diagnostic code for the pain is selected based on the associated general medical condition if one has been established (see Appendix G) or on the anatomical location of the pain if the underlying general medical condition is not yet clearly established—for example, low back (724.2), sciatic (724.3), pelvic (625.9), headache (784.0), facial (784.0), chest (786.50), joint (719.4), bone (733.90), abdominal (789.0), breast (611.71), renal (788.0), ear (388.70), eye (379.91), throat (784.1), tooth (525.9), and urinary (788.0).

■ 300.7 Hypochondriasis

A. Preoccupation with fears of having, or the idea that one has, a serious disease based on the person's misinterpretation of bodily symptoms.

B. The preoccupation persists despite appropriate medical evaluation and reassurance.

C. The belief in Criterion A is not of delusional intensity (as in Delusional Disorder, Somatic Type) and is not restricted to a circumscribed concern about appearance (as in Body Dysmorphic Disorder).

D. The preoccupation causes clinically significant distress or impairment in social, occupational, or other important areas of functioning.

E. The duration of the disturbance is at least 6 months.

F. The preoccupation is not better accounted for by Generalized Anxiety Disorder, Obsessive-Compulsive Disorder, Panic Disorder, a Major Depressive Episode, Separation Anxiety, or another Somatoform Disorder.

Specify if:

> **With Poor Insight:** if, for most of the time during the current episode, the person does not recognize that the concern about having a serious illness is excessive or unreasonable

■ 300.7   Body Dysmorphic Disorder

A. Preoccupation with an imagined defect in appearance. If a slight physical anomaly is present, the person's concern is markedly excessive.

B. The preoccupation causes clinically significant distress or impairment in social, occupational, or other important areas of functioning.

C. The preoccupation is not better accounted for by another mental disorder (e.g., dissatisfaction with body shape and size in Anorexia Nervosa).

■ 300.82 Somatoform Disorder Not Otherwise Specified

This category includes disorders with somatoform symptoms that do not meet the criteria for any specific Somatoform Disorder. Examples include

1. Pseudocyesis: a false belief of being pregnant that is associated with objective signs of pregnancy, which may include abdominal enlargement (although the umbilicus does not become everted), reduced menstrual flow, amenorrhea, subjective sensation of fetal movement, nausea, breast engorgement and secretions, and labor pains at the expected date of delivery. Endocrine changes may be present, but the syndrome cannot be explained by a general medical condition that causes endocrine changes (e.g., a hormone-secreting tumor).
2. A disorder involving nonpsychotic hypochondriacal symptoms of less than 6 months' duration.
3. A disorder involving unexplained physical complaints (e.g., fatigue or body weakness) of less than 6 months' duration that are not due to another mental disorder.

Factitious Disorders

■ Factitious Disorder

A. Intentional production or feigning of physical or psychological signs or symptoms.

B. The motivation for the behavior is to assume the sick role.

C. External incentives for the behavior (such as economic gain, avoiding legal responsibility, or improving physical well-being, as in Malingering) are absent.

Code based on type:

300.16 With Predominantly Psychological Signs and Symptoms: if psychological signs and symptoms predominate in the clinical presentation

300.19 With Predominantly Physical Signs and Symptoms: if physical signs and symptoms predominate in the clinical presentation

300.19 With Combined Psychological and Physical Signs and Symptoms: if both psychological and physical signs and symptoms are present but neither predominates in the clinical presentation

■ 300.19 Factitious Disorder Not Otherwise Specified

This category includes disorders with factitious symptoms that do not meet the criteria for Factitious Disorder. An example is factitious disorder by proxy: the intentional production or feigning of physical or psychological signs or symptoms in another person who is under the individual's care for the purpose of indirectly assuming the sick role (see Appendix B in DSM-IV for suggested research criteria).

Dissociative Disorders

■ 300.12   Dissociative Amnesia
(*formerly* Psychogenic Amnesia)

A. The predominant disturbance is one or more episodes of inability to recall important personal information, usually of a traumatic or stressful nature, that is too extensive to be explained by ordinary forgetfulness.

B. The disturbance does not occur exclusively during the course of Dissociative Identity Disorder, Dissociative Fugue, Posttraumatic Stress Disorder, Acute Stress Disorder, or Somatization Disorder and is not due to the direct physiological effects of a substance (e.g., a drug of abuse, a medication) or a neurological or other general medical condition (e.g., Amnestic Disorder Due to Head Trauma).

C. The symptoms cause clinically significant distress or impairment in social, occupational, or other important areas of functioning.

■ 300.13   Dissociative Fugue
(*formerly* Psychogenic Fugue)

A. The predominant disturbance is sudden, unexpected travel away from home or one's customary place of work, with inability to recall one's past.

B. Confusion about personal identity or assumption of a new identity (partial or complete).

C. The disturbance does not occur exclusively during the course of Dissociative Identity Disorder and is not due to the direct physiological effects of a substance (e.g., a drug of abuse, a medication) or a general medical condition (e.g., temporal lobe epilepsy).

D. The symptoms cause clinically significant distress or impairment in social, occupational, or other important areas of functioning.

■ 300.14   Dissociative Identity Disorder (*formerly* Multiple Personality Disorder)

A. The presence of two or more distinct identities or personality states (each with its own relatively enduring pattern of perceiving, relating to, and thinking about the environment and self).

B. At least two of these identities or personality states recurrently take control of the person's behavior.

C. Inability to recall important personal information that is too extensive to be explained by ordinary forgetfulness.

D. The disturbance is not due to the direct physiological effects of a substance (e.g., blackouts or chaotic behavior during Alcohol Intoxication) or a general medical condition (e.g., complex partial seizures). **Note:** In children, the symptoms are not attributable to imaginary playmates or other fantasy play.

■ 300.6   Depersonalization Disorder

A. Persistent or recurrent experiences of feeling detached from, and as if one is an outside observer of, one's mental processes or body (e.g., feeling like one is in a dream).

B. During the depersonalization experience, reality testing remains intact.

C. The depersonalization causes clinically significant distress or impairment in social, occupational, or other important areas of functioning.

D. The depersonalization experience does not occur exclusively during the course of another mental disorder, such as Schizophrenia, Panic Disorder, Acute Stress Disorder, or another Dissociative Disorder, and is not due to the direct physiological effects of a substance (e.g., a drug of abuse, a medication) or a general medical condition (e.g., temporal lobe epilepsy).

■ 300.15   Dissociative Disorder Not Otherwise Specified

This category is included for disorders in which the predominant feature is a dissociative symptom (i.e., a disruption in the usually integrated functions of consciousness, memory, identity, or perception of the environment) that does not meet the criteria for any specific Dissociative Disorder. Examples include

1. Clinical presentations similar to Dissociative Identity Disorder that fail to meet full criteria for this disorder. Examples include presentations in which a) there are

not two or more distinct personality states, or b) amnesia for important personal information does not occur.

2. Derealization unaccompanied by depersonalization in adults.

3. States of dissociation that occur in individuals who have been subjected to periods of prolonged and intense coercive persuasion (e.g., brainwashing, thought reform, or indoctrination while captive).

4. Dissociative trance disorder: single or episodic disturbances in the state of consciousness, identity, or memory that are indigenous to particular locations and cultures. Dissociative trance involves narrowing of awareness of immediate surroundings or stereotyped behaviors or movements that are experienced as being beyond one's control. Possession trance involves replacement of the customary sense of personal identity by a new identity, attributed to the influence of a spirit, power, deity, or other person, and associated with stereotyped "involuntary" movements or amnesia. Examples include *amok* (Indonesia), *bebainan* (Indonesia), *latah* (Malaysia), *pibloktoq* (Arctic), *ataque de nervios* (Latin America), and possession (India). The dissociative or trance disorder is not a normal part of a broadly accepted collective cultural or religious practice. (See Appendix B in DSM-IV for suggested research criteria.)

5. Loss of consciousness, stupor, or coma not attributable to a general medical condition.

6. Ganser syndrome: the giving of approximate answers to questions (e.g., "2 plus 2 equals 5") when not associated with Dissociative Amnesia or Dissociative Fugue.

Sexual and Gender Identity Disorders

This section includes criteria sets for Sexual Dysfunctions, Paraphilias, and Gender Identity Disorder.

Sexual Dysfunctions

Specific subtypes that apply to all primary Sexual Dysfunctions are listed on p. 238. These subtypes may be used to describe onset, context, and etiological factors.

Sexual Desire Disorders

■ 302.71   Hypoactive Sexual Desire Disorder

A. Persistently or recurrently deficient (or absent) sexual fantasies and desire for sexual activity. The judgment of deficiency or absence is made by the clinician, taking into account factors that affect sexual functioning, such as age and the context of the person's life.

B. The disturbance causes marked distress or interpersonal difficulty.

C. The sexual dysfunction is not better accounted for by another Axis I disorder (except another Sexual Dysfunction) and is not due exclusively to the direct physiological effects of a substance (e.g., a drug of abuse, a medication) or a general medical condition.

■ 302.79 Sexual Aversion Disorder

A. Persistent or recurrent extreme aversion to, and avoidance of, all (or almost all) genital sexual contact with a sexual partner.

B. The disturbance causes marked distress or interpersonal difficulty.

C. The sexual dysfunction is not better accounted for by another Axis I disorder (except another Sexual Dysfunction).

Sexual Arousal Disorders

■ 302.72 Female Sexual Arousal Disorder

A. Persistent or recurrent inability to attain, or to maintain until completion of the sexual activity, an adequate lubrication-swelling response of sexual excitement.

B. The disturbance causes marked distress or interpersonal difficulty.

C. The sexual dysfunction is not better accounted for by another Axis I disorder (except another Sexual Dysfunction) and is not due exclusively to the direct physiological effects of a substance (e.g., a drug of abuse, a medication) or a general medical condition.

■ 302.72 Male Erectile Disorder

A. Persistent or recurrent inability to attain, or to maintain until completion of the sexual activity, an adequate erection.

B. The disturbance causes marked distress or interpersonal difficulty.

C. The erectile dysfunction is not better accounted for by another Axis I disorder (other than a Sexual Dysfunction) and is not due exclusively to the direct physiological effects of a substance (e.g., a drug of abuse, a medication) or a general medical condition.

Orgasmic Disorders

■ 302.73 Female Orgasmic Disorder (*formerly* Inhibited Female Orgasm)

A. Persistent or recurrent delay in, or absence of, orgasm following a normal sexual excitement phase. Women exhibit wide variability in the type or intensity of stimulation that triggers orgasm. The diagnosis of Female Orgasmic Disorder should be based on the clinician's judgment that the woman's orgasmic capacity is less than would be reasonable for her age, sexual experience, and the adequacy of sexual stimulation she receives.

B. The disturbance causes marked distress or interpersonal difficulty.

C. The orgasmic dysfunction is not better accounted for by another Axis I disorder (except another Sexual Dysfunction) and is not due exclusively to the direct physiological effects of a substance (e.g., a drug of abuse, a medication) or a general medical condition.

■ 302.74 Male Orgasmic Disorder (*formerly Inhibited Male Orgasm*)

A. Persistent or recurrent delay in, or absence of, orgasm following a normal sexual excitement phase during sexual activity that the clinician, taking into account the person's age, judges to be adequate in focus, intensity, and duration.

B. The disturbance causes marked distress or interpersonal difficulty.

C. The orgasmic dysfunction is not better accounted for by another Axis I disorder (except another Sexual Dysfunction) and is not due exclusively to the direct physiological effects of a substance (e.g., a drug of abuse, a medication) or a general medical condition.

■ 302.75 Premature Ejaculation

A. Persistent or recurrent ejaculation with minimal sexual stimulation before, on, or shortly after penetration and before the person wishes it. The clinician must take into account factors that affect duration of the excitement phase, such as age, novelty of the sexual partner or situation, and recent frequency of sexual activity.

B. The disturbance causes marked distress or interpersonal difficulty.

C. The premature ejaculation is not due exclusively to the direct effects of a substance (e.g., withdrawal from opioids).

Sexual Pain Disorders

■ 302.76 Dyspareunia (Not Due to a General Medical Condition)

A. Recurrent or persistent genital pain associated with sexual intercourse in either a male or a female.

B. The disturbance causes marked distress or interpersonal difficulty.

C. The disturbance is not caused exclusively by Vaginismus or lack of lubrication, is not better accounted for by another Axis I disorder (except another Sexual Dysfunction), and is not due exclusively to the direct physiological effects of a substance (e.g., a drug of abuse, a medication) or a general medical condition.

■ 306.51 Vaginismus (Not Due to a General Medical Condition)

A. Recurrent or persistent involuntary spasm of the musculature of the outer third of the vagina that interferes with sexual intercourse.

B. The disturbance causes marked distress or interpersonal difficulty.

C. The disturbance is not better accounted for by another Axis I disorder (e.g., Somatization Disorder) and is not due exclusively to the direct physiological effects of a general medical condition.

Subtypes

The following subtypes apply to all primary Sexual Dysfunctions.

One of the following subtypes may be used to indicate the nature of the onset of the Sexual Dysfunction:

Lifelong Type: if the sexual dysfunction has been present since the onset of sexual functioning.

Acquired Type: if the sexual dysfunction develops only after a period of normal functioning.

One of the following subtypes may be used to indicate the context in which the Sexual Dysfunction occurs:

Generalized Type: if the sexual dysfunction is not limited to certain types of stimulation, situations, or partners.

Situational Type: if the sexual dysfunction is limited to certain types of stimulation, situations, or partners. Although in most instances the dysfunctions occur during sexual activity with a partner, in some cases it may be appropriate to identify dysfunctions that occur during masturbation.

One of the following subtypes may be used to indicate etiological factors associated with the Sexual Dysfunction:

Due to Psychological Factors: when psychological factors are judged to have the major role in the onset, severity, exacerbation, or maintenance of the Sexual Dysfunction, and general medical conditions and substances play no role in the etiology of the Sexual Dysfunction.

Due to Combined Factors: when 1) psychological factors are judged to have a role in the onset, severity, exacerbation, or maintenance of the Sexual Dysfunction; and 2) a general medical condition or substance use is also judged to be contributory but is not sufficient to account for the Sexual Dysfunction. If a general medical condition or substance use (including medication side effects) is sufficient to account for the Sexual Dysfunction, Sexual Dysfunction Due to a General Medical Condition (p. 239) and/or Substance-Induced Sexual Dysfunction (p. 240) is diagnosed.

■ Sexual Dysfunction Due to . . . [Indicate the General Medical Condition]

A. Clinically significant sexual dysfunction that results in marked distress or interpersonal difficulty predominates in the clinical picture.

B. There is evidence from the history, physical examination, or laboratory findings that the sexual dysfunction is fully explained by the direct physiological effects of a general medical condition.

C. The disturbance is not better accounted for by another mental disorder (e.g., Major Depressive Disorder).

Select code and term based on the predominant sexual dysfunction:

625.8 Female Hypoactive Sexual Desire Disorder Due to . . . [Indicate the General Medical Condition]: if deficient or absent sexual desire is the predominant feature

608.89 Male Hypoactive Sexual Desire Disorder Due to . . . *[Indicate the General Medical Condition]:* if deficient or absent sexual desire is the predominant feature

607.84 Male Erectile Disorder Due to . . . *[Indicate the General Medical Condition]:* if male erectile dysfunction is the predominant feature

625.0 Female Dyspareunia Due to . . . *[Indicate the General Medical Condition]:* if pain associated with intercourse is the predominant feature

608.89 Male Dyspareunia Due to . . . *[Indicate the General Medical Condition]:* if pain associated with intercourse is the predominant feature

625.8 Other Female Sexual Dysfunction Due to . . . *[Indicate the General Medical Condition]:* if some other feature is predominant (e.g., Orgasmic Disorder) or no feature predominates

608.89 Other Male Sexual Dysfunction Due to . . . *[Indicate the General Medical Condition]:* if some other feature is predominant (e.g., Orgasmic Disorder) or no feature predominates

Coding note: Include the name of the general medical condition on Axis I, e.g., 607.84 Male Erectile Disorder Due to Diabetes Mellitus; also code the general medical condition on Axis III (see Appendix G for codes).

■ Substance-Induced Sexual Dysfunction

A. Clinically significant sexual dysfunction that results in marked distress or interpersonal difficulty predominates in the clinical picture.

B. There is evidence from the history, physical examination, or laboratory findings that the sexual dysfunction is fully explained by substance use as manifested by either (1) or (2):

(1) the symptoms in Criterion A developed during, or within a month of, Substance Intoxication

(2) medication use is etiologically related to the disturbance

C. The disturbance is not better accounted for by a Sexual Dysfunction that is not substance induced. Evidence that the symptoms are better accounted for by a Sexual Dysfunction that is not substance induced might include the following: the symptoms precede the onset of the substance use or dependence (or medication use); the symptoms persist for a substantial period of time (e.g., about a month) after the cessation of intoxication, or are substantially in excess of what would be expected given the type or amount of the substance used or the duration of use; or there is other evidence that suggests the existence of an independent non-substance-induced Sexual Dysfunction (e.g., a history of recurrent non-substance-related episodes).

Note: This diagnosis should be made instead of a diagnosis of Substance Intoxication only when the sexual dysfunction is in excess of that usually associated with the intoxication syndrome and when the dysfunction is sufficiently severe to warrant independent clinical attention.

Code [Specific Substance]–Induced Sexual Dysfunction:
(291.89 Alcohol; 292.89 Amphetamine [or Amphetamine-Like Substance]; 292.89 Cocaine; 292.89 Opioid; 292.89 Sedative, Hypnotic, or Anxiolytic; 292.89 Other [or Unknown] Substance)

Coding note: See p. 115 for recording procedures.

Specify if:

With Impaired Desire: if deficient or absent sexual desire is the predominant feature

With Impaired Arousal: if impaired sexual arousal (e.g., erectile dysfunction, impaired lubrication) is the predominant feature

With Impaired Orgasm: if impaired orgasm is the predominant feature

With Sexual Pain: if pain associated with intercourse is the predominant feature

Specify if:

With Onset During Intoxication: if the criteria are met for Intoxication with the substance and the symptoms develop during the intoxication syndrome

■ 302.70   Sexual Dysfunction Not Otherwise Specified

This category includes sexual dysfunctions that do not meet criteria for any specific Sexual Dysfunction. Examples include

1. No (or substantially diminished) subjective erotic feelings despite otherwise-normal arousal and orgasm
2. Situations in which the clinician has concluded that a sexual dysfunction is present but is unable to determine whether it is primary, due to a general medical condition, or substance induced

Paraphilias

■ 302.4 Exhibitionism

A. Over a period of at least 6 months, recurrent, intense sexually arousing fantasies, sexual urges, or behaviors involving the exposure of one's genitals to an unsuspecting stranger.

B. The fantasies, sexual urges, or behaviors cause clinically significant distress or impairment in social, occupational, or other important areas of functioning.

■ 302.81 Fetishism

A. Over a period of at least 6 months, recurrent, intense sexually arousing fantasies, sexual urges, or behaviors involving the use of nonliving objects (e.g., female undergarments).

B. The fantasies, sexual urges, or behaviors cause clinically significant distress or impairment in social, occupational, or other important areas of functioning.

C. The fetish objects are not limited to articles of female clothing used in cross-dressing (as in Transvestic Fetishism) or devices designed for the purpose of tactile genital stimulation (e.g., a vibrator).

■ 302.89 Frotteurism

A. Over a period of at least 6 months, recurrent, intense sexually arousing fantasies, sexual urges, or behaviors involving touching and rubbing against a nonconsenting person.

B. The fantasies, sexual urges, or behaviors cause clinically significant distress or impairment in social, occupational, or other important areas of functioning.

■ 302.2 Pedophilia

A. Over a period of at least 6 months, recurrent, intense sexually arousing fantasies, sexual urges, or behaviors involving sexual activity with a prepubescent child or children (generally age 13 years or younger).

B. The fantasies, sexual urges, or behaviors cause clinically significant distress or impairment in social, occupational, or other important areas of functioning.

C. The person is at least age 16 years and at least 5 years older than the child or children in Criterion A.

Note: Do not include an individual in late adolescence involved in an ongoing sexual relationship with a 12- or 13-year-old.

Specify if:
Sexually Attracted to Males
Sexually Attracted to Females
Sexually Attracted to Both

Specify if:
Limited to Incest

S*pecify* type:
>**Exclusive Type** (attracted only to children)
>**Nonexclusive Type**

■ 302.83 Sexual Masochism

A. Over a period of at least 6 months, recurrent, intense sexually arousing fantasies, sexual urges, or behaviors involving the act (real, not simulated) of being humiliated, beaten, bound, or otherwise made to suffer.

B. The fantasies, sexual urges, or behaviors cause clinically significant distress or impairment in social, occupational, or other important areas of functioning.

■ 302.84 Sexual Sadism

A. Over a period of at least 6 months, recurrent, intense sexually arousing fantasies, sexual urges, or behaviors involving acts (real, not simulated) in which the psychological or physical suffering (including humiliation) of the victim is sexually exciting to the person.

B. The fantasies, sexual urges, or behaviors cause clinically significant distress or impairment in social, occupational, or other important areas of functioning.

■ 302.3 Transvestic Fetishism

A. Over a period of at least 6 months, in a heterosexual male, recurrent, intense sexually arousing fantasies, sexual urges, or behaviors involving cross-dressing.

B. The fantasies, sexual urges, or behaviors cause clinically significant distress or impairment in social, occupational, or other important areas of functioning.

Specify if:

> **With Gender Dysphoria:** if the person has persistent
> discomfort with gender role or identity

■ 302.82 Voyeurism

A. Over a period of at least 6 months, recurrent, intense
    sexually arousing fantasies, sexual urges, or behaviors
    involving the act of observing an unsuspecting person
    who is naked, in the process of disrobing, or engaging
    in sexual activity.

B. The fantasies, sexual urges, or behaviors cause clinically
    significant distress or impairment in social, occupa-
    tional, or other important areas of functioning.

■ 302.9 Paraphilia Not Otherwise Specified

This category is included for coding Paraphilias that do not
meet the criteria for any of the specific categories. Examples
include, but are not limited to, telephone scatologia (ob-
scene phone calls), necrophilia (corpses), partialism (exclusive focus on part of body), zoophilia (animals), coprophilia
(feces), klismaphilia (enemas), and urophilia (urine).

Gender Identity Disorders

■ Gender Identity Disorder

A. A strong and persistent cross-gender identification (not
    merely a desire for any perceived cultural advantages of
    being the other sex).

In children, the disturbance is manifested by four (or more) of the following:

(1)   repeatedly stated desire to be, or insistence that he or she is, the other sex

(2)   in boys, preference for cross-dressing or simulating female attire; in girls, insistence on wearing only stereotypical masculine clothing

(3)   strong and persistent preferences for cross-sex roles in make-believe play or persistent fantasies of being the other sex

(4)   intense desire to participate in the stereotypical games and pastimes of the other sex

(5)   strong preference for playmates of the other sex

In adolescents and adults, the disturbance is manifested by symptoms such as a stated desire to be the other sex, frequent passing as the other sex, desire to live or be treated as the other sex, or the conviction that he or she has the typical feelings and reactions of the other sex.

B.   Persistent discomfort with his or her sex or sense of inappropriateness in the gender role of that sex.

In children, the disturbance is manifested by any of the following: in boys, assertion that his penis or testes are disgusting or will disappear or assertion that it would be better not to have a penis, or aversion toward rough-and-tumble play and rejection of male stereotypical toys, games, and activities; in girls, rejection of urinating in a sitting position, assertion that she has or will grow a penis, or assertion that she does not want to grow breasts or menstruate, or marked aversion toward normative feminine clothing.

In adolescents and adults, the disturbance is manifested by symptoms such as preoccupation with getting rid of primary and secondary sex characteristics (e.g., request for hormones, surgery, or other procedures to physically alter sexual characteristics to simulate the other sex) or belief that he or she was born the wrong sex.

C. The disturbance is not concurrent with a physical intersex condition.

D. The disturbance causes clinically significant distress or impairment in social, occupational, or other important areas of functioning.

Code based on current age:
    302.6   Gender Identity Disorder in Children
    302.85   Gender Identity Disorder in Adolescents or Adults

Specify if (for sexually mature individuals):
    Sexually Attracted to Males
    Sexually Attracted to Females
    Sexually Attracted to Both
    Sexually Attracted to Neither

■ 302.6   Gender Identity Disorder Not Otherwise Specified

This category is included for coding disorders in gender identity that are not classifiable as a specific Gender Identity Disorder. Examples include

1. Intersex conditions (e.g., androgen insensitivity syndrome or congenital adrenal hyperplasia) and accompanying gender dysphoria

2. Transient, stress-related cross-dressing behavior
3. Persistent preoccupation with castration or penectomy without a desire to acquire the sex characteristics of the other sex

■ 302.9   Sexual Disorder Not Otherwise Specified

This category is included for coding a sexual disturbance that does not meet the criteria for any specific Sexual Disorder and is neither a Sexual Dysfunction nor a Paraphilia. Examples include

1. Marked feelings of inadequacy concerning sexual performance or other traits related to self-imposed standards of masculinity or femininity
2. Distress about a pattern of repeated sexual relationships involving a succession of lovers who are experienced by the individual only as things to be used
3. Persistent and marked distress about sexual orientation

Eating Disorders

■ 307.1   Anorexia Nervosa

A. Refusal to maintain body weight at or above a minimally normal weight for age and height (e.g., weight loss leading to maintenance of body weight less than 85% of that expected; or failure to make expected weight gain during period of growth, leading to body weight less than 85% of that expected).

B. Intense fear of gaining weight or becoming fat, even though underweight.

C. Disturbance in the way in which one's body weight or shape is experienced, undue influence of body weight or shape on self-evaluation, or denial of the seriousness of the current low body weight.

D. In postmenarcheal females, amenorrhea, i.e., the absence of at least three consecutive menstrual cycles. (A woman is considered to have amenorrhea if her periods occur only following hormone, e.g., estrogen, administration.)

Specify type:

  Restricting Type: during the current episode of Anorexia Nervosa, the person has not regularly engaged in binge-eating or purging behavior (i.e., self-induced vomiting or the misuse of laxatives, diuretics, or enemas)

Binge-Eating/Purging Type: during the current episode of Anorexia Nervosa, the person has regularly engaged in binge-eating or purging behavior (i.e., self-induced vomiting or the misuse of laxatives, diuretics, or enemas)

■ 307.51   Bulimia Nervosa

A.   Recurrent episodes of binge eating. An episode of binge eating is characterized by both of the following:

(1)   eating, in a discrete period of time (e.g., within any 2-hour period), an amount of food that is definitely larger than most people would eat during a similar period of time and under similar circumstances

(2)   a sense of lack of control over eating during the episode (e.g., a feeling that one cannot stop eating or control what or how much one is eating)

B.   Recurrent inappropriate compensatory behavior in order to prevent weight gain, such as self-induced vomiting; misuse of laxatives, diuretics, enemas, or other medications; fasting; or excessive exercise.

C.   The binge eating and inappropriate compensatory behaviors both occur, on average, at least twice a week for 3 months.

D.   Self-evaluation is unduly influenced by body shape and weight.

E.   The disturbance does not occur exclusively during episodes of Anorexia Nervosa.

S*pecify* type:

Purging Type: during the current episode of Bulimia Nervosa, the person has regularly engaged in self-induced vomiting or the misuse of laxatives, diuretics, or enemas

Nonpurging Type: during the current episode of Bulimia Nervosa, the person has used other inappropriate compensatory behaviors, such as fasting or excessive exercise, but has not regularly engaged in self-induced vomiting or the misuse of laxatives, diuretics, or enemas

■ 307.50   Eating Disorder Not Otherwise Specified

The Eating Disorder Not Otherwise Specified category is for disorders of eating that do not meet the criteria for any specific Eating Disorder. Examples include

1. For females, all of the criteria for Anorexia Nervosa are met except that the individual has regular menses.
2. All of the criteria for Anorexia Nervosa are met except that, despite significant weight loss, the individual's current weight is in the normal range.
3. All of the criteria for Bulimia Nervosa are met except that the binge eating and inappropriate compensatory mechanisms occur at a frequency of less than twice a week or for a duration of less than 3 months.
4. The regular use of inappropriate compensatory behavior by an individual of normal body weight after eating small amounts of food (e.g., self-induced vomiting after the consumption of two cookies).
5. Repeatedly chewing and spitting out, but not swallowing, large amounts of food.

6. Binge-eating disorder: recurrent episodes of binge eating in the absence of the regular use of inappropriate compensatory behaviors characteristic of Bulimia Nervosa (see Appendix B in DSM-IV for suggested research criteria).

Sleep Disorders

Primary Sleep Disorders

Dyssomnias

■ 307.42   Primary Insomnia

A. The predominant complaint is difficulty initiating or maintaining sleep, or nonrestorative sleep, for at least 1 month.

B. The sleep disturbance (or associated daytime fatigue) causes clinically significant distress or impairment in social, occupational, or other important areas of functioning.

C. The sleep disturbance does not occur exclusively during the course of Narcolepsy, Breathing-Related Sleep Disorder, Circadian Rhythm Sleep Disorder, or a Parasomnia.

D. The disturbance does not occur exclusively during the course of another mental disorder (e.g., Major Depressive Disorder, Generalized Anxiety Disorder, a delirium).

E. The disturbance is not due to the direct physiological effects of a substance (e.g., a drug of abuse, a medication) or a general medical condition.

■ 307.44 Primary Hypersomnia

A. The predominant complaint is excessive sleepiness for at least 1 month (or less if recurrent) as evidenced by either prolonged sleep episodes or daytime sleep episodes that occur almost daily.

B. The excessive sleepiness causes clinically significant distress or impairment in social, occupational, or other important areas of functioning.

C. The excessive sleepiness is not better accounted for by insomnia and does not occur exclusively during the course of another Sleep Disorder (e.g., Narcolepsy, Breathing-Related Sleep Disorder, Circadian Rhythm Sleep Disorder, or a Parasomnia) and cannot be accounted for by an inadequate amount of sleep.

D. The disturbance does not occur exclusively during the course of another mental disorder.

E. The disturbance is not due to the direct physiological effects of a substance (e.g., a drug of abuse, a medication) or a general medical condition.

Specify if:
Recurrent: if there are periods of excessive sleepiness that last at least 3 days occurring several times a year for at least 2 years

■ 347 Narcolepsy

A. Irresistible attacks of refreshing sleep that occur daily over at least 3 months.

B. The presence of one or both of the following:
    (1) cataplexy (i.e., brief episodes of sudden bilateral loss of muscle tone, most often in association with intense emotion)
    (2) recurrent intrusions of elements of rapid eye movement (REM) sleep into the transition between sleep and wakefulness, as manifested by either hypnopompic or hypnagogic hallucinations or sleep paralysis at the beginning or end of sleep episodes

C. The disturbance is not due to the direct physiological effects of a substance (e.g., a drug of abuse, a medication) or another general medical condition.

■ 780.59 Breathing-Related Sleep Disorder

A. Sleep disruption, leading to excessive sleepiness or insomnia, that is judged to be due to a sleep-related breathing condition (e.g., obstructive or central sleep apnea syndrome or central alveolar hypoventilation syndrome).

B. The disturbance is not better accounted for by another mental disorder and is not due to the direct physiological effects of a substance (e.g., a drug of abuse, a medication) or another general medical condition (other than a breathing-related disorder).

Coding note: Also code sleep-related breathing disorder on Axis III.

■ 307.45 Circadian Rhythm Sleep Disorder (*formerly* Sleep-Wake Schedule Disorder)

A. A persistent or recurrent pattern of sleep disruption leading to excessive sleepiness or insomnia that is due to a mismatch between the sleep-wake schedule required by a person's environment and his or her circadian sleep-wake pattern.

B. The sleep disturbance causes clinically significant distress or impairment in social, occupational, or other important areas of functioning.

C. The disturbance does not occur exclusively during the course of another Sleep Disorder or other mental disorder.

D. The disturbance is not due to the direct physiological effects of a substance (e.g., a drug of abuse, a medication) or a general medical condition.

Specify type:

Delayed Sleep Phase Type: a persistent pattern of late sleep onset and late awakening times, with an inability to fall asleep and awaken at a desired earlier time

Jet Lag Type: sleepiness and alertness that occur at an inappropriate time of day relative to local time, occurring after repeated travel across more than one time zone

Shift Work Type: insomnia during the major sleep period or excessive sleepiness during the major awake period associated with night shift work or frequently changing shift work

Unspecified Type (e.g., advanced sleep phase, non-24-hour sleep-wake pattern, irregular sleep-wake pattern, or other unspecified pattern)

■ 307.47   Dyssomnia Not Otherwise Specified

The Dyssomnia Not Otherwise Specified category is for insomnias, hypersomnias, or circadian rhythm disturbances that do not meet criteria for any specific Dyssomnia. Examples include

1. Complaints of clinically significant insomnia or hypersomnia that are attributable to environmental factors (e.g., noise, light, frequent interruptions).

2. Excessive sleepiness that is attributable to ongoing sleep deprivation.

3. Idiopathic "Restless Legs Syndrome": uncomfortable sensations (e.g., discomfort, crawling sensations, or restlessness) that lead to an intense urge to move the legs. Typically, the sensations begin in the evening before sleep onset and are temporarily relieved by moving the legs or walking, only to begin again when the legs are immobile. The sensations can delay sleep onset or awaken the individual from sleep.

4. Idiopathic periodic limb movements ("nocturnal myoclonus"): repeated low-amplitude brief limb jerks, particularly in the lower extremities. These movements begin near sleep onset and decrease during stage 3 or 4 non–rapid eye movement (NREM) and rapid eye movement (REM) sleep. Movements usually occur rhythmically every 20–60 seconds, leading to repeated, brief arousals. Individuals are typically unaware of the actual movements, but may complain of insomnia, frequent awakenings, or daytime sleepiness if the number of movements is very large.

5. Situations in which the clinician has concluded that a Dyssomnia is present but is unable to determine whether it is primary, due to a general medical condition, or substance induced.

Parasomnias

■ 307.47 Nightmare Disorder (*formerly* Dream Anxiety Disorder)

A. Repeated awakenings from the major sleep period or naps with detailed recall of extended and extremely frightening dreams, usually involving threats to survival, security, or self-esteem. The awakenings generally occur during the second half of the sleep period.

B. On awakening from the frightening dreams, the person rapidly becomes oriented and alert (in contrast to the confusion and disorientation seen in Sleep Terror Disorder and some forms of epilepsy).

C. The dream experience, or the sleep disturbance resulting from the awakening, causes clinically significant distress or impairment in social, occupational, or other important areas of functioning.

D. The nightmares do not occur exclusively during the course of another mental disorder (e.g., a delirium, Posttraumatic Stress Disorder) and are not due to the direct physiological effects of a substance (e.g., a drug of abuse, a medication) or a general medical condition.

■ 307.46   Sleep Terror Disorder

A.   Recurrent episodes of abrupt awakening from sleep, usually occurring during the first third of the major sleep episode and beginning with a panicky scream.

B.   Intense fear and signs of autonomic arousal, such as tachycardia, rapid breathing, and sweating, during each episode.

C.   Relative unresponsiveness to efforts of others to comfort the person during the episode.

D.   No detailed dream is recalled and there is amnesia for the episode.

E.   The episodes cause clinically significant distress or impairment in social, occupational, or other important areas of functioning.

F.   The disturbance is not due to the direct physiological effects of a substance (e.g., a drug of abuse, a medication) or a general medical condition.

■ 307.46   Sleepwalking Disorder

A.   Repeated episodes of rising from bed during sleep and walking about, usually occurring during the first third of the major sleep episode.

B.   While sleepwalking, the person has a blank, staring face, is relatively unresponsive to the efforts of others to communicate with him or her, and can be awakened only with great difficulty.

C. On awakening (either from the sleepwalking episode or the next morning), the person has amnesia for the episode.

D. Within several minutes after awakening from the sleep-walking episode, there is no impairment of mental activity or behavior (although there may initially be a short period of confusion or disorientation).

E. The sleepwalking causes clinically significant distress or impairment in social, occupational, or other important areas of functioning.

F. The disturbance is not due to the direct physiological effects of a substance (e.g., a drug of abuse, a medica-tion) or a general medical condition.

■ 307.47 Parasomnia Not Otherwise Specified

The Parasomnia Not Otherwise Specified category is for disturbances that are characterized by abnormal behavioral or physiological events during sleep or sleep-wake transi-tions, but that do not meet criteria for a more specific Parasomnia. Examples include

1. REM sleep behavior disorder: motor activity, often of a violent nature, that arises during rapid eye movement (REM) sleep. Unlike sleepwalking, these episodes tend to occur later in the night and are associated with vivid dream recall.

2. Sleep paralysis: an inability to perform voluntary move-ment during the transition between wakefulness and sleep. The episodes may occur at sleep onset (hypna-gogic) or with awakening (hypnopompic). The epi-

sodes are usually associated with extreme anxiety and, in some cases, fear of impending death. Sleep paralysis occurs commonly as an ancillary symptom of Narcolepsy and, in such cases, should not be coded separately.

3. Situations in which the clinician has concluded that a Parasomnia is present but is unable to determine whether it is primary, due to a general medical condition, or substance induced.

Sleep Disorders Related to Another Mental Disorder

■ **307.42   Insomnia Related to . . .**
[*Indicate the Axis I or Axis II disorder*]

A. The predominant complaint is difficulty initiating or maintaining sleep, or nonrestorative sleep, for at least 1 month that is associated with daytime fatigue or impaired daytime functioning.

B. The sleep disturbance (or daytime sequelae) causes clinically significant distress or impairment in social, occupational, or other important areas of functioning.

C. The insomnia is judged to be related to another Axis I or Axis II disorder (e.g., Major Depressive Disorder, Generalized Anxiety Disorder, Adjustment Disorder With Anxiety), but is sufficiently severe to warrant independent clinical attention.

D. The disturbance is not better accounted for by another Sleep Disorder (e.g., Narcolepsy, Breathing-Related Sleep Disorder, a Parasomnia).

E. The disturbance is not due to the direct physiological effects of a substance (e.g., a drug of abuse, a medication) or a general medical condition.

■ 307.44   Hypersomnia Related to . . . [*Indicate the* Axis I *or* Axis II *disorder*]

A. The predominant complaint is excessive sleepiness for at least 1 month as evidenced by either prolonged sleep episodes or daytime sleep episodes that occur almost daily.

B. The excessive sleepiness causes clinically significant distress or impairment in social, occupational, or other important areas of functioning.

C. The hypersomnia is judged to be related to another Axis I or Axis II disorder (e.g., Major Depressive Disorder, Dysthymic Disorder), but is sufficiently severe to warrant independent clinical attention.

D. The disturbance is not better accounted for by another Sleep Disorder (e.g., Narcolepsy, Breathing-Related Sleep Disorder, a Parasomnia) or by an inadequate amount of sleep.

E. The disturbance is not due to the direct physiological effects of a substance (e.g., a drug of abuse, a medication) or a general medical condition.

Other Sleep Disorders

■ 780.xx Sleep Disorder Due to . . . [*Indicate the General Medical Condition*]

A. A prominent disturbance in sleep that is sufficiently severe to warrant independent clinical attention.

B. There is evidence from the history, physical examination, or laboratory findings that the sleep disturbance is the direct physiological consequence of a general medical condition.

C. The disturbance is not better accounted for by another mental disorder (e.g., an Adjustment Disorder in which the stressor is a serious medical illness).

D. The disturbance does not occur exclusively during the course of a delirium.

E. The disturbance does not meet the criteria for Breathing-Related Sleep Disorder or Narcolepsy.

F. The sleep disturbance causes clinically significant distress or impairment in social, occupational, or other important areas of functioning.

Specify type:
.52 **Insomnia Type:** if the predominant sleep disturbance is insomnia
.54 **Hypersomnia Type:** if the predominant sleep disturbance is hypersomnia
.59 **Parasomnia Type:** if the predominant sleep disturbance is a Parasomnia

.59 Mixed Type: if more than one sleep disturbance
   is present and none predominates

Coding note: Include the name of the general medical condition
on Axis I, e.g., 780.52 Sleep Disorder Due to Chronic Obstructive
Pulmonary Disease, Insomnia Type; also code the general medical
condition on Axis III (see Appendix G for codes).

■ Substance-Induced Sleep Disorder

A. A prominent disturbance in sleep that is sufficiently
   severe to warrant independent clinical attention.

B. There is evidence from the history, physical examination, or laboratory findings of either (1) or (2):

   (1) the symptoms in Criterion A developed during, or
        within a month of, Substance Intoxication or With-
        drawal
   (2) medication use is etiologically related to the sleep
        disturbance

C. The disturbance is not better accounted for by a Sleep
   Disorder that is not substance induced. Evidence that
   the symptoms are better accounted for by a Sleep
   Disorder that is not substance induced might include the
   following: the symptoms precede the onset of the
   substance use (or medication use); the symptoms persist
   for a substantial period of time (e.g., about a month)
   after the cessation of acute withdrawal or severe intoxication, or are substantially in excess of what would be
   expected given the type or amount of the substance
   used or the duration of use; or there is other evidence
   that suggests the existence of an independent non-
   substance-induced Sleep Disorder (e.g., a history of
   recurrent non-substance-related episodes).

D. The disturbance does not occur exclusively during the course of a delirium.

E. The sleep disturbance causes clinically significant distress or impairment in social, occupational, or other important areas of functioning.

Note: This diagnosis should be made instead of a diagnosis of Substance Intoxication or Substance Withdrawal only when the sleep symptoms are in excess of those usually associated with the intoxication or withdrawal syndrome and when the symptoms are sufficiently severe to warrant independent clinical attention.

Code [Specific Substance]–Induced Sleep Disorder:
(291.89 Alcohol; 292.89 Amphetamine; 292.89 Caffeine; 292.89 Cocaine; 292.89 Opioid; 292.89 Sedative, Hypnotic, or Anxiolytic; 292.89 Other [or Unknown] Substance)

Coding note: See p. 115 for recording procedures.

Specify type:
Insomnia Type: if the predominant sleep disturbance is insomnia
Hypersomnia Type: if the predominant sleep disturbance is hypersomnia
Parasomnia Type: if the predominant sleep disturbance is a Parasomnia
Mixed Type: if more than one sleep disturbance is present and none predominates

Specify if (see table on p. 106 for applicability by substance):
With Onset During Intoxication: if the criteria are met for Intoxication with the substance and the symptoms develop during the intoxication syndrome
With Onset During Withdrawal: if criteria are met for Withdrawal from the substance and the symptoms develop during, or shortly after, a withdrawal syndrome

Impulse-Control Disorders Not Elsewhere Classified

■ 312.34   Intermittent Explosive Disorder

A. Several discrete episodes of failure to resist aggressive impulses that result in serious assaultive acts or destruction of property.

B. The degree of aggressiveness expressed during the episodes is grossly out of proportion to any precipitating psychosocial stressors.

C. The aggressive episodes are not better accounted for by another mental disorder (e.g., Antisocial Personality Disorder, Borderline Personality Disorder, a Psychotic Disorder, a Manic Episode, Conduct Disorder, or Attention-Deficit/Hyperactivity Disorder) and are not due to the direct physiological effects of a substance (e.g., a drug of abuse, a medication) or a general medical condition (e.g., head trauma, Alzheimer's disease).

■ 312.32   Kleptomania

A. Recurrent failure to resist impulses to steal objects that are not needed for personal use or for their monetary value.

B. Increasing sense of tension immediately before committing the theft.

C. Pleasure, gratification, or relief at the time of committing the theft.

D. The stealing is not committed to express anger or vengeance and is not in response to a delusion or a hallucination.

E. The stealing is not better accounted for by Conduct Disorder, a Manic Episode, or Antisocial Personality Disorder.

■ 312.33   Pyromania

A. Deliberate and purposeful fire setting on more than one occasion.

B. Tension or affective arousal before the act.

C. Fascination with, interest in, curiosity about, or attraction to fire and its situational contexts (e.g., paraphernalia, uses, consequences).

D. Pleasure, gratification, or relief when setting fires, or when witnessing or participating in their aftermath.

E. The fire setting is not done for monetary gain, as an expression of sociopolitical ideology, to conceal criminal activity, to express anger or vengeance, to improve one's living circumstances, in response to a delusion or hallucination, or as a result of impaired judgment (e.g., in dementia, Mental Retardation, Substance Intoxication).

F. The fire setting is not better accounted for by Conduct Disorder, a Manic Episode, or Antisocial Personality Disorder.

■ 312.31   Pathological Gambling

A. Persistent and recurrent maladaptive gambling behavior
    as indicated by five (or more) of the following:

    (1) is preoccupied with gambling (e.g., preoccupied
    with reliving past gambling experiences, handi-
    capping or planning the next venture, or thinking
    of ways to get money with which to gamble)

    (2) needs to gamble with increasing amounts of
    money in order to achieve the desired excitement

    (3) has repeated unsuccessful efforts to control, cut
    back, or stop gambling

    (4) is restless or irritable when attempting to cut
    down or stop gambling

    (5) gambles as a way of escaping from problems or
    of relieving a dysphoric mood (e.g., feelings of
    helplessness, guilt, anxiety, depression)

    (6) after losing money gambling, often returns an-
    other day to get even ("chasing" one's losses)

    (7) lies to family members, therapist, or others to
    conceal the extent of involvement with gambling

    (8) has committed illegal acts such as forgery, fraud,
    theft, or embezzlement to finance gambling

    (9) has jeopardized or lost a significant relationship,
    job, or educational or career opportunity because
    of gambling

    (10) relies on others to provide money to relieve a
    desperate financial situation caused by gambling

B. The gambling behavior is not better accounted for by a
    Manic Episode.

■ 312.39   Trichotillomania

A. Recurrent pulling out of one's hair resulting in noticeable hair loss.

B. An increasing sense of tension immediately before pulling out the hair or when attempting to resist the behavior.

C. Pleasure, gratification, or relief when pulling out the hair.

D. The disturbance is not better accounted for by another mental disorder and is not due to a general medical condition (e.g., a dermatological condition).

E. The disturbance causes clinically significant distress or impairment in social, occupational, or other important areas of functioning.

■ 312.30   Impulse-Control Disorder Not Otherwise Specified

This category is for disorders of impulse control that do not meet the criteria for any specific Impulse-Control Disorder or for another mental disorder having features involving impulse control described elsewhere in the manual (e.g., Substance Dependence, a Paraphilia).

Adjustment Disorders

■ Adjustment Disorders

A. The development of emotional or behavioral symptoms in response to an identifiable stressor(s) occurring within 3 months of the onset of the stressor(s).

B. These symptoms or behaviors are clinically significant as evidenced by either of the following:
   (1) marked distress that is in excess of what would be expected from exposure to the stressor
   (2) significant impairment in social or occupational (academic) functioning

C. The stress-related disturbance does not meet the criteria for another specific Axis I disorder and is not merely an exacerbation of a preexisting Axis I or Axis II disorder.

D. The symptoms do not represent Bereavement.

E. Once the stressor (or its consequences) has terminated, the symptoms do not persist for more than an additional 6 months.

Specify if:
    Acute: if the disturbance lasts less than 6 months
    Chronic: if the disturbance lasts for 6 months or longer. By definition, symptoms cannot persist for more than 6 months after the termination of the stressor or its consequences. The Chronic specifier therefore applies when the duration of the distur-

bance is longer than 6 months in response to a chronic stressor or to a stressor that has enduring consequences.

Adjustment Disorders are coded according to the subtype that best characterizes the predominant symptoms:

309.0 With Depressed Mood: when the predominant manifestations are symptoms such as depressed mood, tearfulness, or feelings of hopelessness

309.24 With Anxiety: when the predominant manifestations are symptoms such as nervousness, worry, or jitteriness or, in children, fears of separation from major attachment figures

309.28 With Mixed Anxiety and Depressed Mood: when the predominant manifestation is a combination of depression and anxiety

309.3 With Disturbance of Conduct: when the predominant manifestation is a disturbance in conduct in which there is violation of the rights of others or of major age-appropriate societal norms and rules (e.g., truancy, vandalism, reckless driving, fighting, defaulting on legal responsibilities)

309.4 With Mixed Disturbance of Emotions and Conduct: when the predominant manifestations are both emotional symptoms (e.g., depression, anxiety) and a disturbance of conduct (see above subtype)

309.9 Unspecified: for maladaptive reactions (e.g., physical complaints, social withdrawal, or work or academic inhibition) to psychosocial stressors that are not classifiable as one of the specific subtypes of Adjustment Disorder

Coding note: In a multiaxial assessment, the nature of the stressor can be indicated by listing it on Axis IV (e.g., Divorce).

Personality Disorders

This section begins with a general definition of Personality Disorder that applies to each of the 10 specific Personality Disorders. All Personality Disorders are coded on Axis II.

■ General diagnostic criteria for a Personality Disorder

A. An enduring pattern of inner experience and behavior that deviates markedly from the expectations of the individual's culture. This pattern is manifested in two (or more) of the following areas:

    (1) cognition (i.e., ways of perceiving and interpreting self, other people, and events)

    (2) affectivity (i.e., the range, intensity, lability, and appropriateness of emotional response)

    (3) interpersonal functioning

    (4) impulse control

B. The enduring pattern is inflexible and pervasive across a broad range of personal and social situations.

C. The enduring pattern leads to clinically significant distress or impairment in social, occupational, or other important areas of functioning.

D. The pattern is stable and of long duration and its onset can be traced back at least to adolescence or early adulthood.

E. The enduring pattern is not better accounted for as a manifestation or consequence of another mental disorder.

F. The enduring pattern is not due to the direct physiological effects of a substance (e.g., a drug of abuse, a medication) or a general medical condition (e.g., head trauma).

Cluster A Personality Disorders

■ 301.0 Paranoid Personality Disorder

A. A pervasive distrust and suspiciousness of others such that their motives are interpreted as malevolent, beginning by early adulthood and present in a variety of contexts, as indicated by four (or more) of the following:

   (1) suspects, without sufficient basis, that others are exploiting, harming, or deceiving him or her

   (2) is preoccupied with unjustified doubts about the loyalty or trustworthiness of friends or associates

   (3) is reluctant to confide in others because of unwarranted fear that the information will be used maliciously against him or her

   (4) reads hidden demeaning or threatening meanings into benign remarks or events

   (5) persistently bears grudges, i.e., is unforgiving of insults, injuries, or slights

(6)   perceives attacks on his or her character or reputation that are not apparent to others and is quick to react angrily or to counterattack

(7)   has recurrent suspicions, without justification, regarding fidelity of spouse or sexual partner

B.   Does not occur exclusively during the course of Schizophrenia, a Mood Disorder With Psychotic Features, or another Psychotic Disorder and is not due to the direct physiological effects of a general medical condition.

Note: If criteria are met prior to the onset of Schizophrenia, add "Premorbid," e.g., "Paranoid Personality Disorder (Premorbid)."

■ 301.20   Schizoid Personality Disorder

A.   A pervasive pattern of detachment from social relationships and a restricted range of expression of emotions in interpersonal settings, beginning by early adulthood and present in a variety of contexts, as indicated by four (or more) of the following:

(1)   neither desires nor enjoys close relationships, including being part of a family

(2)   almost always chooses solitary activities

(3)   has little, if any, interest in having sexual experiences with another person

(4)   takes pleasure in few, if any, activities

(5)   lacks close friends or confidants other than first-degree relatives

(6)   appears indifferent to the praise or criticism of others

(7)   shows emotional coldness, detachment, or flattened affectivity

B. Does not occur exclusively during the course of Schizophrenia, a Mood Disorder With Psychotic Features,
another Psychotic Disorder, or a Pervasive Developmental Disorder and is not due to the direct physiological effects of a general medical condition.

Note: If criteria are met prior to the onset of Schizophrenia, add
"Premorbid," e.g., "Schizoid Personality Disorder (Premorbid)."

■ 301.22 Schizotypal Personality Disorder

A. A pervasive pattern of social and interpersonal deficits
marked by acute discomfort with, and reduced capacity
for, close relationships as well as by cognitive or perceptual distortions and eccentricities of behavior, beginning by early adulthood and present in a variety of
contexts, as indicated by five (or more) of the following:

(1) ideas of reference (excluding delusions of reference)

(2) odd beliefs or magical thinking that influences
behavior and is inconsistent with subcultural
norms (e.g., superstitiousness, belief in clairvoy-
ance, telepathy, or "sixth sense"; in children and
adolescents, bizarre fantasies or preoccupations)

(3) unusual perceptual experiences, including bodily
illusions

(4) odd thinking and speech (e.g., vague, circumstan-
tial, metaphorical, overelaborate, or stereotyped)

(5) suspiciousness or paranoid ideation

(6) inappropriate or constricted affect

(7) behavior or appearance that is odd, eccentric, or
peculiar

(8) lack of close friends or confidants other than
first-degree relatives

(9)   excessive social anxiety that does not diminish with familiarity and tends to be associated with paranoid fears rather than negative judgments about self

B. Does not occur exclusively during the course of Schizophrenia, a Mood Disorder With Psychotic Features, another Psychotic Disorder, or a Pervasive Developmental Disorder.

Note: If criteria are met prior to the onset of Schizophrenia, add "Premorbid," e.g., "Schizotypal Personality Disorder (Premorbid)."

Cluster B Personality Disorders

■ 301.7   Antisocial Personality Disorder

A. There is a pervasive pattern of disregard for and violation of the rights of others occurring since age 15 years, as indicated by three (or more) of the following:

(1)   failure to conform to social norms with respect to lawful behaviors as indicated by repeatedly performing acts that are grounds for arrest

(2)   deceitfulness, as indicated by repeated lying, use of aliases, or conning others for personal profit or pleasure

(3)   impulsivity or failure to plan ahead

(4)   irritability and aggressiveness, as indicated by repeated physical fights or assaults

(5)   reckless disregard for safety of self or others

(6)   consistent irresponsibility, as indicated by repeated failure to sustain consistent work behavior or honor financial obligations

    (7)   lack of remorse, as indicated by being indifferent to or rationalizing having hurt, mistreated, or stolen from another

B. The individual is at least age 18 years.

C. There is evidence of Conduct Disorder (see p. 66) with onset before age 15 years.

D. The occurrence of antisocial behavior is not exclusively during the course of Schizophrenia or a Manic Episode.

■ 301.83 Borderline Personality Disorder

A pervasive pattern of instability of interpersonal relationships, self-image, and affects, and marked impulsivity beginning by early adulthood and present in a variety of contexts, as indicated by five (or more) of the following:

    (1)   frantic efforts to avoid real or imagined abandonment. **Note:** Do not include suicidal or self-mutilating behavior covered in Criterion 5.

    (2)   a pattern of unstable and intense interpersonal relationships characterized by alternating between extremes of idealization and devaluation

    (3)   identity disturbance: markedly and persistently unstable self-image or sense of self

    (4)   impulsivity in at least two areas that are potentially self-damaging (e.g., spending, sex, substance abuse, reckless driving, binge eating). **Note:** Do not include suicidal or self-mutilating behavior covered in Criterion 5.

    (5)   recurrent suicidal behavior, gestures, or threats, or self-mutilating behavior

(6)   affective instability due to a marked reactivity of mood (e.g., intense episodic dysphoria, irritability, or anxiety usually lasting a few hours and only rarely more than a few days)

(7)   chronic feelings of emptiness

(8)   inappropriate, intense anger or difficulty controlling anger (e.g., frequent displays of temper, constant anger, recurrent physical fights)

(9)   transient, stress-related paranoid ideation or severe dissociative symptoms

■ 301.50 Histrionic Personality Disorder

A pervasive pattern of excessive emotionality and attention seeking, beginning by early adulthood and present in a variety of contexts, as indicated by five (or more) of the following:

(1)   is uncomfortable in situations in which he or she is not the center of attention

(2)   interaction with others is often characterized by inappropriate sexually seductive or provocative behavior

(3)   displays rapidly shifting and shallow expression of emotions

(4)   consistently uses physical appearance to draw attention to self

(5)   has a style of speech that is excessively impressionistic and lacking in detail

(6)   shows self-dramatization, theatricality, and exaggerated expression of emotion

(7)   is suggestible, i.e., easily influenced by others or circumstances

(8)   considers relationships to be more intimate than they actually are

■ 301.81   Narcissistic Personality Disorder

A pervasive pattern of grandiosity (in fantasy or behavior), need for admiration, and lack of empathy, beginning by early adulthood and present in a variety of contexts, as indicated by five (or more) of the following:

(1)   has a grandiose sense of self-importance (e.g., exaggerates achievements and talents, expects to be recognized as superior without commensurate achievements)

(2)   is preoccupied with fantasies of unlimited success, power, brilliance, beauty, or ideal love

(3)   believes that he or she is "special" and unique and can only be understood by, or should associate with, other special or high-status people (or institutions)

(4)   requires excessive admiration

(5)   has a sense of entitlement, i.e., unreasonable expectations of especially favorable treatment or automatic compliance with his or her expectations

(6)   is interpersonally exploitative, i.e., takes advantage of others to achieve his or her own ends

(7)   lacks empathy: is unwilling to recognize or identify with the feelings and needs of others

(8)   is often envious of others or believes that others are envious of him or her

(9)   shows arrogant, haughty behaviors or attitudes

Cluster C Personality Disorders

■ 301.82 Avoidant Personality Disorder

A pervasive pattern of social inhibition, feelings of inadequacy, and hypersensitivity to negative evaluation, beginning by early adulthood and present in a variety of contexts, as indicated by four (or more) of the following:

(1) avoids occupational activities that involve significant interpersonal contact, because of fears of criticism, disapproval, or rejection

(2) is unwilling to get involved with people unless certain of being liked

(3) shows restraint within intimate relationships because of the fear of being shamed or ridiculed

(4) is preoccupied with being criticized or rejected in social situations

(5) is inhibited in new interpersonal situations because of feelings of inadequacy

(6) views self as socially inept, personally unappealing, or inferior to others

(7) is unusually reluctant to take personal risks or to engage in any new activities because they may prove embarrassing

■ 301.6 Dependent Personality Disorder

A pervasive and excessive need to be taken care of that leads to submissive and clinging behavior and fears of separation, beginning by early adulthood and present in a variety of contexts, as indicated by five (or more) of the following:

(1) has difficulty making everyday decisions without an excessive amount of advice and reassurance from others

(2) needs others to assume responsibility for most major areas of his or her life

(3) has difficulty expressing disagreement with others because of fear of loss of support or approval. **Note:** Do not include realistic fears of retribution.

(4) has difficulty initiating projects or doing things on his or her own (because of a lack of self-confidence in judgment or abilities rather than a lack of motivation or energy)

(5) goes to excessive lengths to obtain nurturance and support from others, to the point of volunteering to do things that are unpleasant

(6) feels uncomfortable or helpless when alone because of exaggerated fears of being unable to care for himself or herself

(7) urgently seeks another relationship as a source of care and support when a close relationship ends

(8) is unrealistically preoccupied with fears of being left to take care of himself or herself

■ 301.4 Obsessive-Compulsive Personality Disorder

A pervasive pattern of preoccupation with orderliness, perfectionism, and mental and interpersonal control, at the expense of flexibility, openness, and efficiency, beginning by early adulthood and present in a variety of contexts, as indicated by four (or more) of the following:

(1) is preoccupied with details, rules, lists, order, organization, or schedules to the extent that the major point of the activity is lost

(2) shows perfectionism that interferes with task completion (e.g., is unable to complete a project because his or her own overly strict standards are not met)

(3) is excessively devoted to work and productivity to the exclusion of leisure activities and friendships (not accounted for by obvious economic necessity)

(4) is overconscientious, scrupulous, and inflexible about matters of morality, ethics, or values (not accounted for by cultural or religious identification)

(5) is unable to discard worn-out or worthless objects even when they have no sentimental value

(6) is reluctant to delegate tasks or to work with others unless they submit to exactly his or her way of doing things

(7) adopts a miserly spending style toward both self and others; money is viewed as something to be hoarded for future catastrophes

(8) shows rigidity and stubbornness

■ 301.9   Personality Disorder Not Otherwise Specified

This category is for disorders of personality functioning that do not meet criteria for any specific Personality Disorder. An example is the presence of features of more than one specific Personality Disorder that do not meet the full criteria for any one Personality Disorder ("mixed personality"), but that together cause clinically significant distress or impairment in one or more important areas of functioning (e.g., social or occupational). This category can also be used when the clinician judges that a specific Personality Disorder that is not included in the Classification is appropriate. Examples include depressive personality disorder and passive-aggressive personality disorder (see Appendix B in DSM-IV for suggested research criteria).

Other Conditions That May Be a Focus of Clinical Attention

This section covers other conditions or problems that may be a focus of clinical attention. These are related to the mental disorders described previously in this manual in one of the following ways: 1) the problem is the focus of diagnosis or treatment and the individual has no mental disorder (e.g., a Partner Relational Problem in which neither partner has symptoms that meet criteria for a mental disorder, in which case only the Partner Relational Problem is coded); 2) the individual has a mental disorder but it is unrelated to the problem (e.g., a Partner Relational Problem in which one of the partners has an incidental Specific Phobia, in which case both can be coded); 3) the individual has a mental disorder that is related to the problem, but the problem is sufficiently severe to warrant independent clinical attention (e.g., a Partner Relational Problem sufficiently problematic to be a focus of treatment that is also associated with Major Depressive Disorder in one of the partners, in which case both can be coded). The conditions and problems in this section are coded on Axis I.

Psychological Factors Affecting Medical Condition

■ **316 . . . [Specified Psychological Factor] Affecting . . . [Indicate the General Medical Condition]**

A. A general medical condition (coded on Axis III) is present.

B. Psychological factors adversely affect the general medical condition in one of the following ways:

  (1) the factors have influenced the course of the general medical condition as shown by a close temporal association between the psychological factors and the development or exacerbation of, or delayed recovery from, the general medical condition

  (2) the factors interfere with the treatment of the general medical condition

  (3) the factors constitute additional health risks for the individual

  (4) stress-related physiological responses precipitate or exacerbate symptoms of the general medical condition

Choose name based on the nature of the psychological factors (if more than one factor is present, indicate the most prominent):

  Mental Disorder Affecting . . . [Indicate the General Medical Condition] (e.g., an Axis I disorder such as Major Depressive Disorder delaying recovery from a myocardial infarction)

Psychological Symptoms Affecting . . . [Indicate the General Medical Condition] (e.g., depressive symptoms delaying recovery from surgery; anxiety exacerbating asthma)

Personality Traits or Coping Style Affecting . . . [Indicate the General Medical Condition] (e.g., pathological denial of the need for surgery in a patient with cancer; hostile, pressured behavior contributing to cardiovascular disease)

Maladaptive Health Behaviors Affecting . . . [Indicate the General Medical Condition] (e.g., overeating; lack of exercise; unsafe sex)

Stress-Related Physiological Response Affecting . . . [Indicate the General Medical Condition] (e.g., stress-related exacerbations of ulcer, hypertension, arrhythmia, or tension headache)

Other or Unspecified Psychological Factors Affecting . . . [Indicate the General Medical Condition] (e.g., interpersonal, cultural, or religious factors)

Medication-Induced Movement Disorders

The following Medication-Induced Movement Disorders are included because of their frequent importance in 1) the management by medication of mental disorders or general medical conditions; and 2) the differential diagnosis with Axis I disorders (e.g., Anxiety Disorder versus Neuroleptic-Induced Akathisia; catatonia versus Neuroleptic Malignant Syndrome). Although these disorders are labeled "medication induced," it is often difficult to establish the causal relationship between medication exposure and the development of the movement disorder, especially because some of these movement disorders also occur in the absence of medication exposure. The term *neuroleptic* is used broadly in this manual to refer to medications with dopamine-antagonist properties. These include so-called "typical" antipsychotic agents (e.g., chlorpromazine, haloperidol, fluphenazine), "atypical" antipsychotic agents (e.g., clozapine), certain dopamine receptor blocking drugs used in the treatment of symptoms such as nausea and gastroparesis (e.g., prochlorperazine, promethazine, trimethobenzamide, thiethylperazine, and metoclopramide), and amoxapine, which is marketed as an antidepressant. Medication-Induced Movement Disorders should be coded on Axis I.

■ **332.1   Neuroleptic-Induced Parkinsonism**

Parkinsonian tremor, muscular rigidity, or akinesia developing within a few weeks of starting or raising the dose of a neuroleptic medication (or after reducing a medication used to treat extrapyramidal symptoms). (See Appendix B in DSM-IV for suggested research criteria.)

■ **333.92   Neuroleptic Malignant Syndrome**

Severe muscle rigidity, elevated temperature, and other related findings (e.g., diaphoresis, dysphagia, incontinence, changes in level of consciousness ranging from confusion to coma, mutism, elevated or labile blood pressure, elevated creatine phosphokinase [CPK]) developing in association with the use of neuroleptic medication. (See Appendix B in DSM-IV for suggested research criteria.)

■ **333.7   Neuroleptic-Induced Acute Dystonia**

Abnormal positioning or spasm of the muscles of the head, neck, limbs, or trunk developing within a few days of starting or raising the dose of a neuroleptic medication (or after reducing a medication used to treat extrapyramidal symptoms). (See Appendix B in DSM-IV for suggested research criteria.)

■ 333.99   Neuroleptic-Induced Acute Akathisia

Subjective complaints of restlessness accompanied by observed movements (e.g., fidgety movements of the legs, rocking from foot to foot, pacing, or inability to sit or stand still) developing within a few weeks of starting or raising the dose of a neuroleptic medication (or after reducing a medication used to treat extrapyramidal symptoms). (See Appendix B in DSM-IV for suggested research criteria.)

■ 333.82   Neuroleptic-Induced Tardive Dyskinesia

Involuntary choreiform, athetoid, or rhythmic movements (lasting at least a few weeks) of the tongue, jaw, or extremities developing in association with the use of neuroleptic medication for at least a few months (may be for a shorter period of time in elderly persons). (See Appendix B in DSM-IV for suggested research criteria.)

■ 333.1   Medication-Induced Postural Tremor

Fine tremor occurring during attempts to maintain a posture that develops in association with the use of medication (e.g., lithium, antidepressants, valproate). (See Appendix B in DSM-IV for suggested research criteria.)

■ 333.90 Medication-Induced Movement Disorder Not Otherwise Specified

This category is for Medication-Induced Movement Disorders not classified by any of the specific disorders listed above. Examples include 1) parkinsonism, acute akathisia, acute dystonia, or dyskinetic movement that is associated with a medication other than a neuroleptic; 2) a presentation that resembles neuroleptic malignant syndrome that is associated with a medication other than a neuroleptic; or 3) tardive dystonia.

Other Medication-Induced Disorder

■ 995.2 Adverse Effects of Medication Not Otherwise Specified

This category is available for optional use by clinicians to code side effects of medication (other than movement symptoms) when these adverse effects become a main focus of clinical attention. Examples include severe hypotension, cardiac arrhythmias, and priapism.

Relational Problems

Relational problems include patterns of interaction between or among members of a relational unit that are associated with clinically significant impairment in functioning, or symptoms among one or more members of the relational unit, or impairment in the functioning of the relational unit itself. The following relational problems are included because they are frequently a focus of clinical attention among individuals seen by health professionals. These problems may exacerbate or complicate the management of a mental disorder or general medical condition in one or more members of the relational unit, may be a result of a mental disorder or a general medical condition, may be independent of other conditions that are present, or can occur in the absence of any other condition. When these problems are the principal focus of clinical attention, they should be listed on Axis I. Otherwise, if they are present but not the principal focus of clinical attention, they may be listed on Axis IV. The relevant category is generally applied to all members of a relational unit who are being treated for the problem.

■ V61.9   Relational Problem Related to a Mental Disorder or General Medical Condition

This category should be used when the focus of clinical attention is a pattern of impaired interaction that is associated with a mental disorder or a general medical condition in a family member.

■ V61.20   Parent-Child Relational Problem

This category should be used when the focus of clinical attention is a pattern of interaction between parent and child (e.g., impaired communication, overprotection, inadequate discipline) that is associated with clinically significant impairment in individual or family functioning or the development of clinically significant symptoms in parent or child.

■ V61.10   Partner Relational Problem

This category should be used when the focus of clinical attention is a pattern of interaction between spouses or partners characterized by negative communication (e.g., criticisms), distorted communication (e.g., unrealistic expectations), or noncommunication (e.g., withdrawal) that is associated with clinically significant impairment in individual or family functioning or the development of symptoms in one or both partners.

■ V61.8   Sibling Relational Problem

This category should be used when the focus of clinical attention is a pattern of interaction among siblings that is associated with clinically significant impairment in individual or family functioning or the development of symptoms in one or more of the siblings.

■ V62.81   Relational Problem Not Otherwise Specified

This category should be used when the focus of clinical attention is on relational problems that are not classifiable by any of the specific problems listed above (e.g., difficulties with co-workers).

Problems Related to Abuse or Neglect

This section includes categories that should be used when the focus of clinical attention is severe mistreatment of one individual by another through physical abuse, sexual abuse, or child neglect. These problems are included because they are frequently a focus of clinical attention among individuals seen by health professionals. The appropriate V code applies if the focus of attention is on the perpetrator of the abuse or neglect or on the relational unit in which it occurs. If the individual being evaluated or treated is the victim of the abuse or neglect, code 995.52, 995.53, or 995.54 for a child or 995.81 or 995.83 for an adult (depending on the type of abuse).

■ V61.21 Physical Abuse of Child

This category should be used when the focus of clinical attention is physical abuse of a child.
Coding note: *Code* **995.54** *if focus of clinical attention is on the victim.*

■ V61.21 Sexual Abuse of Child

This category should be used when the focus of clinical attention is sexual abuse of a child.
Coding note: *Code* **995.53** *if focus of clinical attention is on the victim.*

■ V61.21 Neglect of Child

This category should be used when the focus of clinical attention is child neglect.
Coding note: *Code* **995.52** *if focus of clinical attention is on the victim.*

■ **Physical Abuse of Adult**

This category should be used when the focus of clinical attention is physical abuse of an adult (e.g., spouse beating, abuse of elderly parent).

Coding note: *Code*

V61.12 *if focus of clinical attention is on the perpetrator and abuse is by partner*

V62.83 *if focus of clinical attention is on the perpetrator and abuse is by person other than partner*

995.81 *if focus of clinical attention is on the victim*

■ **Sexual Abuse of Adult**

This category should be used when the focus of clinical attention is sexual abuse of an adult (e.g., sexual coercion, rape).

Coding note: *Code*

V61.12 *if focus of clinical attention is on the perpetrator and abuse is by partner*

V62.83 *if focus of clinical attention is on the perpetrator and abuse is by person other than partner*

995.83 *if focus of clinical attention is on the victim*

Additional Conditions That May Be a Focus of Clinical Attention

■ **V15.81   Noncompliance With Treatment**

This category can be used when the focus of clinical attention is noncompliance with an important aspect of the treatment for a mental disorder or a general medical condition. The reasons for noncompliance may include discomfort resulting from treatment (e.g., medication side effects), expense of treatment, decisions based on personal value judgments or religious or cultural beliefs about the advantages and disadvantages of the proposed treatment, maladaptive personality traits or coping styles (e.g., denial of illness), or the presence of a mental disorder (e.g., Schizophrenia, Avoidant Personality Disorder). This category should be used only when the problem is sufficiently severe to warrant independent clinical attention.

■ V65.2   Malingering

The essential feature of Malingering is the intentional production of false or grossly exaggerated physical or psychological symptoms, motivated by external incentives such as avoiding military duty, avoiding work, obtaining financial compensation, evading criminal prosecution, or obtaining drugs. Under some circumstances, Malingering may represent adaptive behavior—for example, feigning illness while a captive of the enemy during wartime.

Malingering should be strongly suspected if any combination of the following is noted:

1. Medicolegal context of presentation (e.g., the person is referred by an attorney to the clinician for examination)
2. Marked discrepancy between the person's claimed stress or disability and the objective findings
3. Lack of cooperation during the diagnostic evaluation and in complying with the prescribed treatment regimen
4. The presence of Antisocial Personality Disorder

Malingering differs from Factitious Disorder in that the motivation for the symptom production in Malingering is an external incentive, whereas in Factitious Disorder external incentives are absent. Evidence of an intrapsychic need to maintain the sick role suggests Factitious Disorder. Malingering is differentiated from Conversion Disorder and other Somatoform Disorders by the intentional production of symptoms and by the obvious, external incentives associated with it. In Malingering (in contrast to Conversion Disorder), symptom relief is not often obtained by suggestion or hypnosis.

■ V71.01   Adult Antisocial Behavior

This category can be used when the focus of clinical attention is adult antisocial behavior that is not due to a mental disorder (e.g., Conduct Disorder, Antisocial Personality Disorder, or an Impulse-Control Disorder). Examples include the behavior of some professional thieves, racketeers, or dealers in illegal substances.

■ V71.02   Child or Adolescent Antisocial Behavior

This category can be used when the focus of clinical attention is antisocial behavior in a child or adolescent that is not due to a mental disorder (e.g., Conduct Disorder or an Impulse-Control Disorder). Examples include isolated antisocial acts of children or adolescents (not a pattern of antisocial behavior).

■ V62.89   Borderline Intellectual Functioning

This category can be used when the focus of clinical attention is associated with borderline intellectual functioning, that is, an IQ in the 71–84 range. Differential diagnosis between Borderline Intellectual Functioning and Mental Retardation (an IQ of 70 or below) is especially difficult when the coexistence of certain mental disorders (e.g., Schizophrenia) is involved.

Coding note: *This is coded on Axis II.*

■ 780.9   Age-Related Cognitive Decline

This category can be used when the focus of clinical attention is an objectively identified decline in cognitive functioning consequent to the aging process that is within normal limits given the person's age. Individuals with this condition may report problems remembering names or appointments or may experience difficulty in solving complex problems. This category should be considered only after it has been determined that the cognitive impairment is not attributable to a specific mental disorder or neurological condition.

■ V62.82   Bereavement

This category can be used when the focus of clinical attention is a reaction to the death of a loved one. As part of their reaction to the loss, some grieving individuals present with symptoms characteristic of a Major Depressive Episode (e.g., feelings of sadness and associated symptoms such as insomnia, poor appetite, and weight loss). The bereaved individual typically regards the depressed mood as "normal," although the person may seek professional help for relief of associated symptoms such as insomnia or anorexia. The duration and expression of "normal" bereavement vary considerably among different cultural groups. The diagnosis of Major Depressive Disorder is generally not given unless the symptoms are still present 2 months after the loss. However, the presence of certain symptoms that are not characteristic of a "normal" grief reaction may be helpful in differentiating bereavement from a Major Depressive Episode. These include 1) guilt about things other than actions taken or not taken by the survivor at the time of the death; 2) thoughts of death other than the survivor feeling that he or she would be better off dead or should have died with the deceased person; 3) morbid preoccupation with worthlessness; 4) marked psychomotor retardation; 5) prolonged and marked functional impairment; and 6) hallucinatory experiences other than thinking that he or she hears the voice of, or transiently sees the image of, the deceased person.

■ V62.3   Academic Problem

This category can be used when the focus of clinical attention is an academic problem that is not due to a mental disorder or, if due to a mental disorder, is sufficiently severe to warrant independent clinical attention. An example is a pattern of failing grades or of significant underachievement in a person with adequate intellectual capacity in the absence of a Learning or Communication Disorder or any other mental disorder that would account for the problem.

■ V62.2   Occupational Problem

This category can be used when the focus of clinical attention is an occupational problem that is not due to a mental disorder or, if it is due to a mental disorder, is sufficiently severe to warrant independent clinical attention. Examples include job dissatisfaction and uncertainty about career choices.

■ 313.82   Identity Problem

This category can be used when the focus of clinical attention is uncertainty about multiple issues relating to identity such as long-term goals, career choice, friendship patterns, sexual orientation and behavior, moral values, and group loyalties.

■ V62.89   Religious or Spiritual Problem

This category can be used when the focus of clinical attention is a religious or spiritual problem. Examples include distressing experiences that involve loss or questioning of faith, problems associated with conversion to a new faith, or questioning of spiritual values that may not necessarily be related to an organized church or religious institution.

■ V62.4   Acculturation Problem

This category can be used when the focus of clinical attention is a problem involving adjustment to a different culture (e.g., following migration).

■ V62.89   Phase of Life Problem

This category can be used when the focus of clinical attention is a problem associated with a particular developmental phase or some other life circumstance that is not due to a mental disorder or, if it is due to a mental disorder, is sufficiently severe to warrant independent clinical attention. Examples include problems associated with entering school, leaving parental control, starting a new career, and changes involved in marriage, divorce, and retirement.

Additional Codes

■ 300.9   Unspecified Mental Disorder (nonpsychotic)

There are several circumstances in which it may be appropriate to assign this code: 1) for a specific mental disorder not included in the DSM-IV Classification, 2) when none of the available Not Otherwise Specified categories is appropriate, or 3) when it is judged that a nonpsychotic mental disorder is present but there is not enough information available to diagnose one of the categories provided in the Classification. In some cases, the diagnosis can be changed to a specific disorder after more information is obtained.

■ V71.09   No Diagnosis or Condition on Axis I

When no Axis I diagnosis or condition is present, this should be indicated. There may or may not be an Axis II diagnosis.

■ 799.9   Diagnosis or Condition Deferred on Axis I

When there is insufficient information to make any diagnostic judgment about an Axis I diagnosis or condition, this should be noted as Diagnosis or Condition Deferred on Axis I.

■ V71.09   No Diagnosis on Axis II

When no Axis II diagnosis (e.g., no Personality Disorder) is present, this should be indicated. There may or may not be an Axis I diagnosis or condition.

■ 799.9   Diagnosis Deferred on Axis II

When there is insufficient information to make any diagnostic judgment about an Axis II diagnosis, this should be noted as Diagnosis Deferred on Axis II.

Listing of
DSM-IV Appendixes

Appendix G: "ICD-9-CM Codes for Selected General Medical Conditions and Medication-Induced Disorders" is included here for convenience in coding. Please see DSM-IV for the following appendixes:

Dissociative trance disorder
Binge-eating disorder
Depressive personality disorder
Passive-aggressive personality disorder
    (negativistic personality disorder)
Medication-Induced Movement Disorders
    Neuroleptic-Induced Parkinsonism
    Neuroleptic Malignant Syndrome
    Neuroleptic-Induced Acute Dystonia
    Neuroleptic-Induced Acute Akathisia
    Neuroleptic-Induced Tardive Dyskinesia
    Medication-Induced Postural Tremor
    Medication-Induced Movement
        Disorder Not Otherwise Specified
Defensive Functioning Scale
Global Assessment of Relational
    Functioning (GARF) Scale
Social and Occupational Functioning
    Assessment Scale (SOFAS)

Appendix G

ICD-9-CM Codes for Selected General Medical Conditions and Medication-Induced Disorders

The official coding system in use as of the publication of DSM-IV is the *International Classification of Diseases,* 9th Revision, Clinical Modification (ICD-9-CM). This appendix contains two sections that are provided to facilitate ICD-9-CM coding: 1) codes for selected general medical conditions, and 2) codes for medication-induced disorders.

ICD-9-CM Codes for Selected General Medical Conditions

The codes specified for use on Axis I and Axis II of DSM-IV represent only a small fraction of the codes provided in ICD-9-CM. The conditions classified outside the "Mental Disorders" chapter of ICD-9-CM are also important for clinical diagnosis and management in mental health settings. Axis III is provided to facilitate the reporting of these conditions (see p. 39). To assist clinicians in finding the ICD-9-CM codes, this appendix provides a selective index of those ICD-9-CM codes for general medical conditions that are most relevant to diagnosis and care in mental health settings. ICD-9-CM offers diagnostic specificity beyond that reflected in many of the codes that appear in this appendix (e.g., to denote a specific anatomical site or the presence of a specific complication). In cases in which increased specificity is noted in the fifth digit of the code, the least specific code (usually "0") has been selected. For example, the code for lymphosarcoma is given as 200.10 (for unspecified site), although more specificity with regard to anatomical site can be noted in the other fifth-digit codes, for example, 200.12 lymphosarcoma, intrathoracic lymph nodes. In cases in which increased specificity is reflected in the fourth digit of the code, this appendix often provides the "unspecified" category (e.g., 555.9 is listed for regional enteritis; ICD-9-CM also includes 555.0 for enteritis involving the small intestine, 555.1 for involvement of the large intestine, and 555.2 for involvement of both). Diagnostic codes for which more specificity is available are indicated in this appendix by an asterisk (*). Clinicians interested in recording greater specificity should refer to the complete listing of codes published in the ICD-9-CM Diseases: Tabular List (Volume 1) and the ICD-9-CM Diseases: Alphabetic Index (Volume 2). These documents are updated every October and are published by the U.S. Department of Health and Human Services. They are available from the Superintendent of Documents, U.S. Government Printing Office, as well as from a number of private publishers.

> **Note:** An asterisk (*) following the ICD-9-CM code indicates that greater specificity (e.g., a specific complication or anatomical site) is available. Refer to the ICD-9-CM Diseases: Tabular List (Volume 1) entry for that code for additional information.

Diseases of the Nervous System

324.0	Abscess, intracranial
331.0	Alzheimer's disease
437.0	Atherosclerosis, cerebral
354.0	Carpal tunnel syndrome
354.4	Causalgia
334.3	Cerebellar ataxia
850.9*	Concussion
851.80*	Contusion, cerebral
359.1	Dystrophy, Duchenne's muscular
348.5	Edema, cerebral
049.9*	Encephalitis, viral
572.2	Encephalopathy, hepatic
437.2	Encephalopathy, hypertensive
348.3*	Encephalopathy, unspecified
345.10*	Epilepsy, grand mal
345.40*	Epilepsy, partial, with impairment of consciousness (temporal lobe)
345.50*	Epilepsy, partial, without impairment of consciousness (Jacksonian)
345.00*	Epilepsy, petit mal (absences)
346.20	Headache, cluster
432.0	Hemorrhage, extradural, nontraumatic
852.40*	Hemorrhage, extradural, traumatic
431	Hemorrhage, intracerebral, nontraumatic
430	Hemorrhage, subarachnoid, nontraumatic
852.00*	Hemorrhage, subarachnoid, traumatic
432.1	Hemorrhage, subdural, nontraumatic

852.20*	Hemorrhage, subdural, traumatic
333.4	Huntington's chorea
331.3	Hydrocephalus, communicating
331.4	Hydrocephalus, obstructive
435.9*	Ischemic attack, transient
046.1	Creutzfeldt-Jakob disease
046.0	Kuru
046.3	Leukoencephalopathy, progressive multifocal
330.1	Lipidosis, cerebral
320.9*	Meningitis, bacterial (due to unspecified bacterium)
321.0	Meningitis, cryptococcal
054.72	Meningitis, herpes simplex virus
053.0	Meningitis, herpes zoster
321.1*	Meningitis, other fungal
094.2	Meningitis, syphilitic
047.9*	Meningitis, viral (due to unspecified virus)
346.00*	Migraine, classical (with aura)
346.10*	Migraine, common
346.90*	Migraine, unspecified
358.0	Myasthenia gravis
350.1	Neuralgia, trigeminal
337.1	Neuropathy, peripheral autonomic
434.9*	Occlusion, cerebral artery
350.2	Pain, face, atypical
351.0	Palsy, Bell's
343.9*	Palsy, cerebral
335.23	Palsy, pseudobulbar
046.2	Panencephalitis, subacute sclerosing
094.1	Paresis, general
332.0	Parkinson's disease, primary
331.1	Pick's disease
357.9*	Polyneuropathy

348.2	Pseudotumor cerebri (benign intracranial hypertension)
335.20	Sclerosis, amyotrophic lateral
340	Sclerosis, multiple (MS)
345.3	Status, grand mal
345.2	Status, petit mal
345.70	Status, temporal lobe
433.1	Stenosis, carotid artery, without cerebral infarction
436	Stroke (CVA)
330.1	Tay-Sachs disease
333.1	Tremor, benign essential

Diseases of the Circulatory System

413.9*	Angina pectoris
424.1	Aortic valve disorder
440.9*	Atherosclerosis
414.00*	Coronary atherosclerosis
426.10*	Block, atrioventricular
426.3*	Block, left bundle branch
426.4	Block, right bundle branch
427.5	Cardiac arrest
425.5	Cardiomyopathy, alcoholic
425.4*	Cardiomyopathy, idiopathic
416.9*	Chronic pulmonary heart disease
427.9*	Dysrhythmia, cardiac, unspecified
415.19*	Embolism, pulmonary
421.9*	Endocarditis, bacterial
428.0*	Failure, congestive heart
427.31	Fibrillation, atrial
427.41	Fibrillation, ventricular
427.32	Flutter, atrial
427.42	Flutter, ventricular

455.6*	Hemorrhoids
401.9*	Hypertension, essential
402.91*	Hypertensive heart disease with congestive heart failure
402.90*	Hypertensive heart disease without congestive heart failure
403.91*	Hypertensive renal disease with failure
403.90*	Hypertensive renal disease without failure
458.0	Hypotension, orthostatic
410.90*	Infarction, myocardial, acute
424.0	Mitral valve insufficiency (nonrheumatic)
424.0	Mitral valve prolapse
394.0*	Mitral valve stenosis (rheumatic)
423.9*	Pericarditis
443.9*	Peripheral vascular disease
451.9*	Phlebitis/thrombophlebitis
446.0	Polyarteritis nodosa
427.60*	Premature beats
424.3	Pulmonary valve disease (nonrheumatic)
397.1	Pulmonary valve disease, rheumatic
427.0	Tachycardia, paroxysmal supraventricular
427.2	Tachycardia, paroxysmal, unspecified
427.1	Tachycardia, ventricular (paroxysmal)
424.2	Tricuspid valve disease (nonrheumatic)
397.0	Tricuspid valve disease, rheumatic
456.0	Varices, esophageal, with bleeding
456.1	Varices, esophageal, without bleeding
454.9*	Varicose veins, lower extremities

Diseases of the Respiratory System

513.0	Abscess of lung
518.0	Atelectasis
493.20*	Asthma, chronic obstructive

493.90[*]   Asthma, unspecified
494   Bronchiectasis
466.0   Bronchitis, acute
491.21   Bronchitis, obstructive chronic (COPD), with acute exacerbation
491.20   Bronchitis, obstructive chronic (COPD), without acute exacerbation
277.00[*]   Cystic fibrosis
511.9[*]   Effusion, pleural
492.8[*]   Emphysema
518.81[*]   Failure, respiratory
505   Pneumoconiosis
860.4[*]   Pneumohemothorax, traumatic
483.0   Pneumonia, mycoplasma
482.9[*]   Pneumonia, unspecified bacterial
481   Pneumonia, pneumococcal
136.3   Pneumonia, pneumocystis
482.30[*]   Pneumonia, streptococcus
486[*]   Pneumonia, unspecified organism
480.9[*]   Pneumonia, viral
512.8[*]   Pneumothorax, spontaneous
860.0[*]   Pneumothorax, traumatic
011.9[*]   Tuberculosis, pulmonary

Neoplasms

ICD-9-CM diagnostic codes for neoplasms are classified in the table of neoplasms in the ICD-9-CM Alphabetic Index (Volume 2) according to site and degree of malignancy (primary, secondary, in situ, benign, uncertain, unspecified). **Note:** For patients with a personal history of malignant neoplasms that have been surgically removed or eradicated by chemotherapy or radiation therapy, codes V10.0–V10.9 should be used; for specific sites, refer to the Alphabetic

Index (Volume 2) of ICD-9-CM under "History (personal) of, malignant neoplasm."

Listed below are some of the most common codes assigned for neoplasms.

228.02	Hemangioma of brain
201.90*	Hodgkin's disease
176.9*	Kaposi's sarcoma
208.01*	Leukemia, acute, in remission
208.00*	Leukemia, acute
208.11*	Leukemia, chronic, in remission
208.10*	Leukemia, chronic
200.10*	Lymphosarcoma
225.2	Meningioma (cerebral)
203.01	Multiple myeloma, in remission
203.00	Multiple myeloma
225.0	Neoplasm, benign, of brain
211.4	Neoplasm, benign, of colon
195.2	Neoplasm, malignant, abdominal cavity, primary
194.0	Neoplasm, malignant, adrenal gland, primary
188.9*	Neoplasm, malignant, bladder, primary
170.9*	Neoplasm, malignant, bone, primary
198.5	Neoplasm, malignant, bone, secondary
191.9*	Neoplasm, malignant, brain, primary
198.3*	Neoplasm, malignant, brain, secondary
174.9*	Neoplasm, malignant, breast, female, primary
175.9*	Neoplasm, malignant, breast, male, primary
162.9*	Neoplasm, malignant, bronchus, primary
180.9*	Neoplasm, malignant, cervix, primary
153.9*	Neoplasm, malignant, colon, primary
197.5	Neoplasm, malignant, colon, secondary
171.9*	Neoplasm, malignant, connective tissue, primary
150.9*	Neoplasm, malignant, esophagus, primary

152.9*	Neoplasm, malignant, intestine, small, primary
189.0*	Neoplasm, malignant, kidney, primary
155.0	Neoplasm, malignant, liver, primary
197.7	Neoplasm, malignant, liver, secondary
162.9*	Neoplasm, malignant, lung, primary
197.0	Neoplasm, malignant, lung, secondary
196.9*	Neoplasm, malignant, lymph nodes, secondary
172.9*	Neoplasm, malignant, melanoma, primary
183.0*	Neoplasm, malignant, ovary, primary
157.9*	Neoplasm, malignant, pancreas, primary
185	Neoplasm, malignant, prostate, primary
154.1	Neoplasm, malignant, rectum, primary
173.9*	Neoplasm, malignant, skin, primary
151.9*	Neoplasm, malignant, stomach, site unspecified, primary
186.9*	Neoplasm, malignant, testis, primary
193	Neoplasm, malignant, thyroid, primary
179*	Neoplasm, malignant, uterus, primary
237.70*	Neurofibromatosis
227.0	Pheochromocytoma, benign
194.0	Pheochromocytoma, malignant
238.4	Polycythemia vera

Endocrine Diseases

253.0	Acromegaly
255.2	Adrenogenital disorder
259.2	Carcinoid syndrome
255.4	Corticoadrenal insufficiency
255.0	Cushing's syndrome
253.5	Diabetes insipidus
250.00*	Diabetes mellitus, type II/non-insulin-dependent
250.01*	Diabetes mellitus, type I/insulin-dependent
253.2	Dwarfism, pituitary

241.9[*]   Goiter, nontoxic nodular
240.9[*]   Goiter, simple
255.1   Hyperaldosteronism
252.0   Hyperparathyroidism
252.1   Hypoparathyroidism
244.9[*]   Hypothyroidism, acquired
243   Hypothyroidism, congenital
256.9[*]   Ovarian dysfunction
253.2   Panhypopituitarism
259.0   Sexual development and puberty, delayed
259.1   Sexual development and puberty, precocious
257.9[*]   Testicular dysfunction
245.9[*]   Thyroiditis
242.9[*]   Thyrotoxicosis

Nutritional Diseases

265.0   Beriberi
269.3   Calcium deficiency
266.2   Folic acid deficiency
269.3   Iodine deficiency
260   Kwashiorkor
262   Malnutrition, protein-caloric, severe
261   Nutritional marasmus
278.00[*] Obesity
265.2   Pellagra (niacin deficiency)
266.0   Riboflavin deficiency
264.9[*]   Vitamin A deficiency
266.1   Vitamin B_6 deficiency
266.2   Vitamin B_{12} deficiency
267   Vitamin C deficiency
268.9[*]   Vitamin D deficiency
269.1   Vitamin E deficiency
269.0   Vitamin K deficiency

Metabolic Diseases

276.2	Acidosis
276.3	Alkalosis
277.3	Amyloidosis
276.5	Depletion, volume (dehydration)
271.3	Disaccharide malabsorption (lactose intolerance)
276.9*	Electrolyte imbalance
276.6	Fluid overload/retention
274.9*	Gout
275.0	Hemochromatosis
275.4	Hypercalcemia
276.7	Hyperkalemia
276.0	Hypernatremia
275.4	Hypocalcemia
276.8	Hypokalemia
276.1	Hyponatremia
270.1	Phenylketonuria (PKU)
277.1	Porphyria
277.2	Lesch-Nyhan syndrome
275.1	Wilson's disease

Diseases of the Digestive System

540.9*	Appendicitis, acute
578.9*	Bleeding, gastrointestinal
575.0	Cholecystitis, acute
575.11	Cholecystitis, chronic
571.2	Cirrhosis, alcoholic
556.9*	Colitis, ulcerative
564.0	Constipation
555.9*	Crohn's disease
009.2	Diarrhea, infectious

558.9*   Diarrhea, unspecified
562.10   Diverticulitis of colon, unspecified
562.12   Diverticulitis of colon, with hemorrhage
562.11   Diverticulosis of colon, unspecified
562.13   Diverticulosis of colon, with hemorrhage
535.50*   Duodenitis and gastritis
555.9*   Enteritis, regional
535.50*   Gastritis and duodenitis
558.9*   Gastroenteritis
530.1   Esophagitis
571.1   Hepatitis, alcoholic, acute
571.40*   Hepatitis, chronic
573.3*   Hepatitis, toxic (includes drug induced)
070.1*   Hepatitis, viral A
070.30*   Hepatitis, viral B
070.51*   Hepatitis, viral C
560.39*   Impaction, fecal
550.90*   Inguinal hernia
564.1   Irritable bowel syndrome
576.2   Obstruction, bile duct
560.9*   Obstruction, intestinal
577.0   Pancreatitis, acute
577.1   Pancreatitis, chronic
567.9*   Peritonitis
530.1   Reflux, esophageal
530.4   Rupture, esophageal
530.3   Stricture, esophageal
532.30*   Ulcer, duodenal, acute
532.70*   Ulcer, duodenal, chronic
531.30*   Ulcer, gastric, acute
531.70*   Ulcer, gastric, chronic

Genitourinary System Diseases

596.4	Atonic bladder
592.0	Calculus, renal
592.1	Calculus, ureter
592.9*	Calculus, urinary, unspecified
595.9*	Cystitis
625.3	Dysmenorrhea
617.9*	Endometriosis
584.9*	Failure, renal, acute
585	Failure, renal, chronic
403.91*	Failure, renal, hypertensive
586*	Failure, renal, unspecified
218.9*	Fibroid of uterus
580.9*	Glomerulonephritis, acute
600	Hypertrophy, prostatic, benign (BPH)
628.9*	Infertility, female
606.9*	Infertility, male
627.9*	Menopausal or postmenopausal disorder
626.9*	Menstruation, disorder of, and abnormal bleeding
625.2	Mittelschmerz
620.2*	Ovarian cyst
614.9*	Pelvic inflammatory disease (PID)
607.3	Priapism
618.9*	Prolapse, genital
601.9*	Prostatitis
593.3	Stricture, ureteral
598.9*	Stricture, urethral
599.0	Urinary tract infection (UTI)

Hematological Diseases

288.0	Agranulocytosis
287.0	Allergic purpura

284.9* Anemia, aplastic
281.2 Anemia, folate-deficiency
283.9* Anemia, hemolytic, acquired
283.11 Anemia, hemolytic-uremic syndrome
280.9* Anemia, iron-deficiency
283.10 Anemia, nonautoimmune hemolytic, unspecified
283.19 Anemia, other autoimmune hemolytic
281.0 Anemia, pernicious
282.60* Anemia, sickle-cell
286.9* Coagulation defects
288.3 Eosinophilia
282.4 Thalassemia
287.5* Thrombocytopenia

Diseases of the Eye

366.9* Cataract
372.9* Conjunctiva disorder
361.9* Detachment, retinal
365.9* Glaucoma
377.30* Neuritis, optic
379.50* Nystagmus
377.00* Papilledema
369.9* Visual loss

Diseases of the Ear, Nose, and Throat

460   Common cold
389.9* Hearing loss
464.0 Laryngitis, acute
386.00* Ménière's disease
382.9* Otitis media
462   Pharyngitis, acute
477.9* Rhinitis, allergic

461.9[*]   Sinusitis, acute
473.9[*]   Sinusitis, chronic
388.30[*]   Tinnitus, unspecified
463   Tonsillitis, acute

Musculoskeletal System and Connective Tissue Diseases

716.20[*]   Arthritis, allergic
711.90[*]   Arthritis, infective
714.0   Arthritis, rheumatoid
733.40[*]   Aseptic necrosis of bone
710.3   Dermatomyositis
722.91   Disc disorder, intervertebral, cervical
722.93   Disc disorder, intervertebral, lumbar
722.92   Disc disorder, intervertebral, thoracic
733.10[*]   Fracture, pathological
715.90[*]   Osteoarthrosis (osteoarthritis)
730.20[*]   Osteomyelitis
733.00[*]   Osteoporosis
710.1   Scleroderma (systemic sclerosis)
737.30   Scoliosis
710.2   Sjögren's disease
720.0   Spondylitis, ankylosing
710.0   Systemic lupus erythematosus

Diseases of the Skin

704.00[*]   Alopecia
692.9[*]   Dermatitis, contact
693.0[*]   Dermatitis, due to substance (taken internally)
682.9[*]   Cellulitis, unspecified site
695.1   Erythema multiforme
703.0   Ingrowing nail

701.4   Keloid scar
696.1[*]   Psoriasis
707.0   Ulcer, decubitus
708.0   Urticaria, allergic

Congenital Malformations, Deformations, and Chromosomal Abnormalities

749.10[*]   Cleft lip
749.00[*]   Cleft palate
758.3   Cri-du-chat syndrome (antimongolism)
758.0   Down's syndrome
760.71   Fetal alcohol syndrome
751.3   Hirschsprung's disease (congenital colon
         dysfunction)
742.3   Hydrocephalus, congenital
752.7   Indeterminate sex and pseudo-
         hermaphroditism
758.7   Klinefelter's syndrome
759.82   Marfan's syndrome
742.1   Microcephalus
741.90[*]   Spina bifida
750.5   Stenosis, congenital hypertrophic pyloric
760.71   Toxic effects of alcohol
760.75   Toxic effects of cocaine
760.73   Toxic effects of hallucinogens
760.72   Toxic effects of narcotics
760.70   Toxic effects of other substances (including
         medications)
759.5   Tuberous sclerosis
758.6   Turner's syndrome
752.5   Undescended testicle

Diseases of Pregnancy, Childbirth, and the Puerperium

Diagnoses associated with pregnancies can be located in the Alphabetic Index (Volume 2) of ICD-9-CM indented under "Pregnancy, complicated (by)," or "Pregnancy, management affected by." Listed below are some of the most common conditions.

642.00[*] Eclampsia
643.0[*]   Hyperemesis gravidarum, mild
643.0[*]   Hyperemesis gravidarum, with metabolic disturbance
642.0[*]   Pre-eclampsia, mild
642.0[*]   Pre-eclampsia, severe

Infectious Diseases

The following codes represent ICD-9-CM diagnostic codes for infections from specific organisms. Traditionally, codes for organisms from the 041 category are used as secondary codes (e.g., urinary tract infection due to *Escherichia coli* would be coded as 599.0 [primary diagnosis] and 041.4 [secondary diagnosis]).

006.9[*]   Amebiasis
112.5   Candidiasis, disseminated
112.4   Candidiasis, lung
112.0   Candidiasis, mouth
112.2   Candidiasis, other urogenital sites
112.3   Candidiasis, skin and nails
112.9   Candidiasis, unspecified site
112.1   Candidiasis, vulva and vagina
099.41   *Chlamydia trachomatis*
001.9[*]   Cholera

041.83	*Clostridium perfrigens*
114.9*	Coccidioidomycosis
078.1	*Condyloma acuminatum* (viral warts)
079.2	Coxsackie virus
117.5	Cryptococcosis
041.4	*Escherichia coli (E. coli)*
007.1	Giardiasis
098.2*	Gonorrhea
041.5	*Hemophilus influenzae (H. influenzae)*
070.1*	Hepatitis, viral A
070.3*	Hepatitis, viral B
070.51	Hepatitis, viral C
054.9*	Herpes simplex
053.9*	Herpes zoster
115.9*	Histoplasmosis
042	HIV infection (symptomatic)
036.9*	Infection, meningococcal
079.99*	Infection, viral, unspecified
487.1	Influenza, unspecified
487.0	Influenza, with pneumonia
041.3*	*Klebsiella pneumoniae*
088.81	Lyme disease
084.6*	Malaria
075	Mononucleosis
072.9*	Mumps
041.81	*Mycoplasma*
041.2	*Pneumococcus*
041.6	*Proteus*
041.7	*Pseudomonas*
071	Rabies
056.9*	Rubella
003.9*	Salmonella
135	Sarcoidosis

004.9[*]   Shigellosis
041.10[*] *Staphylococcus*
041.00[*] *Streptococcus*
097.9[*]   Syphilis
082.9[*]   Tick-borne rikettsiosis
130.9[*]   Toxoplasmosis
124   Trichinosis
131.9[*]   Trichomoniasis
002.0   Typhoid fever
081.9[*]   Typhus

Overdose

Additional diagnostic codes for overdose/poisoning can be located in the Alphabetic Index (Volume 2) of ICD-9-CM in the table of drugs and chemicals, listed alphabetically by drug in the "Poisoning" column.

965.4   Acetaminophen
962.0   Adrenal cortical steroids
972.4   Amyl/butyl/nitrite
962.1   Androgens and anabolic steroids
971.1   Anticholinergics
969.0   Antidepressants
967.0   Barbiturates
969.4   Benzodiazepine-based tranquilizers
969.2   Butyrophenone-based tranquilizers
967.1   Chloral hydrate
968.5   Cocaine
967.5   Glutethimide
969.6   Hallucinogens/cannabis
962.3   Insulin and antidiabetic agents
967.4   Methaqualone
968.2   Nitrous oxide
970.1   Opioid antagonists

965.00	Opioids
967.2	Paraldehyde
968.3	Phencyclidine
969.1	Phenothiazine-based tranquilizers
965.1	Salicylates
970.9	Stimulants
962.7	Thyroid and thyroid derivatives

Additional Codes for Medication-Induced Disorders

The following are the ICD-9-CM codes for selected medications that may cause Substance-Induced Disorders. They are made available for optional use by clinicians in situations in which these medications, prescribed at therapeutic dose levels, have resulted in one of the following: Substance-Induced Delirium, Substance-Induced Persisting Dementia, Substance-Induced Persisting Amnestic Disorder, Substance-Induced Psychotic Disorder, Substance-Induced Mood Disorder, Substance-Induced Anxiety Disorder, Substance-Induced Sexual Dysfunction, Substance-Induced Sleep Disorder, and Medication-Induced Movement Disorders. When used in multiaxial evaluation, the E-codes should be coded on Axis I immediately following the related disorder. It should be noted that these E-codes do not apply to poisonings or to a medication taken as an overdose.

Example: 292.39   Substance-Induced Mood Disorder,
                             With Depressive Features
                  E932.2   Oral contraceptives

Analgesics and Antipyretics

E935.4   Acetaminophen/phenacetin
E935.1   Methadone
E935.6   Nonsteroidal anti-inflammatory agents
E935.2   Other narcotics (e.g., codeine, meperidine)
E935.3   Salicylates (e.g., aspirin)

Anticonvulsants

E936.3   Carbamazepine
E936.2   Ethosuximide
E937.0   Phenobarbital
E936.1   Phenytoin
E936.3   Valproic acid

Antiparkinsonian Medications

E936.4   Amantadine
E941.1   Benztropine
E933.0   Diphenhydramine
E936.4   L-Dopa

Neuroleptic Medications

E939.2   Butyrophenone-based neuroleptics (e.g.,
          haloperidol)
E939.3   Other neuroleptics (e.g., thiothixene)
E939.1   Phenothiazine-based neuroleptics (e.g.,
          chlorpromazine)

Sedatives, Hypnotics, and Anxiolytics

E937.0   Barbiturates
E939.4   Benzodiazepine-based medications

E937.1   Chloral hydrate
E939.5   Hydroxyzine
E937.2   Paraldehyde

Other Psychotropic Medications

E939.0   Antidepressants
E939.6   Cannabis
E940.1   Opioid antagonists
E939.7   Stimulants (excluding central appetite
          depressants)

Cardiovascular Medications

E942.0   Antiarrhythmic medication (includes
          propranolol)
E942.2   Antilipemic and cholesterol-lowering medication
E942.1   Cardiac glycosides (e.g., digitalis)
E942.4   Coronary vasodilators (e.g., nitrates)
E942.3   Ganglion-blocking agents (pentamethonium)
E942.6   Other antihypertensive agents (e.g., clonidine,
          guanethidine, reserpine)
E942.5   Other vasodilators (e.g., hydralazine)

Primarily Systemic Agents

E933.0   Antiallergic and antiemetic agents (excluding
          phenothiazines, hydroxyzine)
E941.1   Anticholinergics (e.g., atropine) and spasmolytics
E934.2   Anticoagulants
E933.1   Antineoplastic and immunosuppressive drugs
E941.0   Cholinergics (parasympathomimetics)
E941.2   Sympathomimetics (adrenergics)
E933.5   Vitamins (excluding vitamin K)

Medications Acting on Muscles and the Respiratory System

E945.7   Antiasthmatics (aminophylline)
E945.4   Antitussives (e.g., dextromethorphan)
E945.8   Other respiratory drugs
E945.0   Oxytocic agents (ergot alkaloids, prostaglandins)
E945.2   Skeletal muscle relaxants
E945.1   Smooth muscle relaxants (metaproterenol)

Hormones and Synthetic Substitutes

E932.0   Adrenal cortical steroids
E932.1   Anabolic steroids and androgens
E932.8   Antithyroid agents
E932.2   Ovarian hormones (includes oral contraceptives)
E932.7   Thyroid replacements

Diuretics and Mineral and Uric Acid Metabolism Drugs

E944.2   Carbonic acid anhydrase inhibitors
E944.3   Chlorthiazides
E944.0   Mercurial diuretics
E944.4   Other diuretics (furosemide, ethacrynic acid)
E944.1   Purine derivative diuretics
E944.7   Uric acid metabolism drugs (probenecid)

Medications Acting on Muscles and the Respiratory System

E945.7   Antiasthmatics (aminophylline)
E945.4   Antitussives (e.g., dextromethorphan)
E945.8   Other respiratory drugs
E945.0   Oxytocic agents (ergot alkaloids, prostaglandins)
E945.2   Skeletal muscle relaxants
E945.1   Smooth muscle relaxants (metaproterenol)

Hormones and Synthetic Substitutes

E932.0   Adrenal cortical steroids
E932.1   Anabolic steroids and androgens
E932.8   Antithyroid agents
E932.2   Ovarian hormones (includes oral contraceptives)
E932.7   Thyroid replacements

Diuretics and Mineral and Uric Acid Metabolism Drugs

E944.2   Carbonic acid anhydrase inhibitors
E944.3   Chlorthiazides
E944.0   Mercurial diuretics
E944.4   Other diuretics (furosemide, ethacrynic acid)
E944.1   Purine derivative diuretics
E944.7   Uric acid metabolism drugs (probenecid)

Index

N

R

S

V

W